Quantum C

Does the Supernatural Lurk in the Fourth Dimension?

A Scientific and Theological Journey through Quantum Mechanics, Time, and the Fourth Spatial Dimension

Josh Peck

Author of *Disclosure*

Quantum Creation

Does the Supernatural Lurk in the Fourth Dimension?

Scripture taken from the King James Version of the Bible unless otherwise noted.

Book cover designed by Zoey Z. (www.zoeyzanax.webs.com)

All artwork used in this book or on cover are either originally designed/manipulated or are taken from the Wikimedia JPEG 'Commons' unless otherwise noted.

For additional information on the author or the book, please visit www.ministudyministry.com.

ISBN-10: 1499760841

ISBN-13: 978-1499760842

Table of Contents

TABLE OF CONTENTS

Table of Figures

Acknowledgements

This book is dedicated to my wife Christina, who was the first one to introduce me to the fascinating world of quantum physics, and to my two children: Jaklynn and Nathan.

* * *

I have a lot of people to thank for this book; there are far more than I could ever list here, but I will do my best. First off I thank my Lord and Savior Jesus Christ, without whom I could do nothing, let alone put this book together. I also want to thank my family and friends for their continued support, encouragement, and prayer. I would like to give a special thanks to Doug Woodward for providing an extraordinary amount of personal time, advice, encouragement, and friendship throughout the writing of this book. I also want to thank Doug Hamp, Rob Skiba, and Jim Wilhelmsen for providing countless combined hours of prayer and conversation throughout this past year. A big thank you goes out to Zoey Z. for giving me honest feedback throughout the course of writing this book as well as contributing her amazing artistic skills for the book cover. For varying reasons, I would also like to thank Treva Abel, Gonz Shimura, LA Marzulli, Paul Kennedy, Johnny from the Iron Show, Parker J. Cole, Natalina of Extraordinary Intelligence, Chris White, Deeanna Williams, Dr. Ken Johnson, Dr. Mallett, Rob Baxter III, Sam Tate, Amy Geer, and all others who have kept my family and our ministry in prayer.

QUANTUM CREATION

Foreword

By S. Douglas Woodward

I never took physics in school. My first reaction to physics was that it looked like a lot of math, formulas, and story problems. I didn't like any of those things. Math especially made my head hurt.

Instead, I liked history, art, literature, and languages. No doubt that is why I majored in 'Letters'. That obscure major allowed my friends to mock me and joke I had only learned the alphabet at the university. Of course, it really meant I had a degree in 'the humanities.' In other words, I had taken the first step to become 'a man of letters.'

This designation is interesting since it harkens to a laudatory expression from the Middle Ages. It referred to a person that could write letters—that is, correspondences—for his patron. More specifically, a man of letters could read, write, and say things prosaically—sometimes poetically. Nevertheless, we might still wonder why being able to accomplish such seemingly mundane things commended the 'man of letters' to society at large. One supposes it was partly because *being literate* and *capable of expressing oneself clearly* was a rare skill. Since no one had telegraphs, short-wave radios, let alone telephones or email, crafting communication carefully was a particularly strategic skill. The time between expressing yourself and receiving a response was likely many weeks or even months. Saying things poorly, especially undiplomatically, might launch countries into war. 'Misspeaking' in your letters was not easily overcome.

Getting back to physics: despite my innate apprehension for this particular science, through the years I have been drawn to what the character Sheldon in *The Big Bang Theory* asserts is the superior physics—what is known as *theoretical physics.* To make my point plain: I wasn't interested in learning how to calculate the horse power it would take to pull a wagon full of bricks (or better yet, like Busch's Clydesdales, pull a wagon full of beer). Instead, I was vitally intrigued by the nature of *matter, energy, and time*—the building blocks of our universe. Early on, I learned (and the reader may recall) the ancients thought that the most fundamental of elements were earth, wind, water, and fire. Three of those four made for a great singing trio in the twentieth century (I'm referring to *Earth, Wind and Fire*), but serious students of science haven't thought these 'meta-elements' comprised the essentials of nature for many, many centuries.

In the past 200 years or so, scientists began to venture that matter and energy were interrelated. In layman's shorthand, matter was compressed energy, inert, waiting to be released. The widespread use of gunpowder had become common enough proof of that. Consequently, if one could discover a trigger to release the energy in matter, such a one could profit, not just by building more powerful weapons of war, but more pacifically from making energy replace horses (hence the analogy, if not necessity, of quantifying horse power). Furthermore, it had become plain enough that components or elements of matter/energy could be separated and distinguished. The alchemists had known this for centuries (if not millennia) when they sought to turn less valuable metals (like iron) into valuable metals (in particular that precious metal—*gold*). However, there was more to it than just that valuable transformation. The transmutation of 'base metals' into 'fine metals' took on spiritual meaning, becoming an analogue for a natural frame of reference to awaken to the spiritual path of *illumination*. An alchemist sought more than just getting rich through chemistry. He sought to become enlightened. His quest was to grow wise as well as wealthy. Alchemy had both a natural and spiritual meaning.

Similarly, the nature of time and space became a matter of more than physics. With Einstein's famous equation of $e=mc^2$ (energy equals mass times the speed of light squared), the world (especially popular science) became smitten with many crazy (but true) notions that most humans had never thought of before. For one, it became important to recognize that *matter existed within space*. Additionally, matter possessed mass; however, this *mass was connected somehow with its existence within time and space*, and with an added but equally essential aspect *of speed*—involving how fast things travel (like light, radio waves, and maybe someday the real instantiation of the USS Enterprise). It turns out to be significant knowing just how quickly things can get from one place to another.

As a quick aside, space might or might not be 'empty.' There has almost always been a debate about whether the *aether* exists—a medium some scientists speculate lies throughout the cosmos even when there appears to be a totally empty vacuum, without atoms or even tinier particles like bosons and quarks.

Nowadays, we talk about how mass, energy, and even time are 'relative' depending upon how all these factors come together in a particular instance. We even commonly employ the once seemingly nonsensical term of 'space-time'—that our universe, our cosmos (our ordered natural scheme of things) consists of *matter and energy* existing *within this space-time*. We experience *space* (measured by the familiar dimensions of height, length, and depth) and *time* (measured by various types of clocks); but most importantly as the way we experience reality through a continuous sequence of events that constantly goes forward and never backward. To expound further: in this modern depiction of the universe, understanding the conversion of matter into energy, we also have to factor how its motion (its speed, that is) causes it to alter the space-time that surrounds it as well as how it is affected by its surrounding space-time. Objects that go faster acquire more mass than when they are 'standing still.' Massive objects (according to Einsteinium physics theory) even *warp* space-time. Particles (like photons) are bent when they pass through this warped space-time.

Therefore, it has become a common affirmation that our natural *universe is much stranger than we once thought.* This oddness causes many to wonder whether what we once called the 'supernatural' is actually just nature behaving differently than we previously understood. Is the supernatural just buried within invisible aspects of the natural? When it comes to the being we call God, is 'He' part of the parcel of this strange nature or is He existent outside of nature?

Of course, when Einstein started elucidating space-time, he didn't work in a vacuum (no pun intended). He was standing on the shoulders of seventeenth century giants like Gottfried Leibniz and Sir Isaac

Newton. But even before these men co-invented the science (and math) of Calculus; before Newton discovered the dual nature of light (existing as both waves and particles), and most importantly before Newton wrote up his *theory of gravity* (a theory which still works perfectly in all but the most extreme situations), there were others who had considered the relationship of 'dimensions' and the nature of time and eternity. For instance, one was the old sage Maimonides (the great Jewish teacher of the twelfth century who lived in Cordoba, Spain) that made observations that seemed to point the way that others (notably, Einstein) might follow to unlock the secrets of the cosmos. Maimonides postulated there were 13 principles of faith. In several respects, *these principles of faith* also provide the basis for what is called *natural science or natural philosophy.* Indeed, the first four provide a foundation for what we may call a truly biblical cosmology:

1. *The existence of God* (a necessary Being who serves as the foundation all forms of existence).

2. *God's unity and indivisibility into elements* (God is One God, as opposed to a pantheon of gods)

3. *God's spirituality and incorporeality* (He *is* even without a body to instantiate His existence)

4. *God's eternity* (He exists *outside* of time and space).

We could digress into a study of these 'first principles' of cosmology. We won't. But my point is that the great 'natural' philosophers from Plato to Aristotle to Maimonides to Newton (and down to our present day, one thinks of Hawking), seek to understand what if any distinction exists between the 'supernatural' and the 'natural'. Most of us want to grasp what the nature of our universe is: "What are its fundamental laws?" For by knowing these laws we acquire understanding, and probably more to the point, we obtain power over nature (note: such power can be either good or bad—it all depends on how we use this knowledge). For persons like Josh Peck and this author, folk concerned with spiritual realities, we also want to understand 'where' God resides, what the essence of other created spiritual beings like angels or demons might be (if they exist and we assume they do), and whether we can literally 'make sense' of what is beyond our senses.

It is in this manner that Josh Peck, my good friend, has written out his thoughts and placed them before you. Like me, he has an inquisitive mind. He has already traveled down this path trying to understand the 'nature' of both nature and the supernatural. He has done so not only to satisfy himself in order that he may benefit from a better understanding. He has done this to help you, the reader, to learn more about this fascinating connection between the natural and the supernatural too—in hopes that you may better appreciate God and His marvelous creation.

Indeed, the work you have picked up explores this seldom trod path where physics and cosmology intersect. Peck attempts to understand whether there are hints within modern scientific knowledge which open the possibility (if not provability) there are genuine realities beyond our senses we might rightly label *supernatural*. Do the findings of modern physics provide a framework that elucidates the nature of God, of time and eternity, of the natural and the supernatural? Do some supernatural phenomena fit within this framework? Do some realities (perhaps God Himself) still exist beyond the invisible dimensions that modern science postulates?

To be sure, Peck ventures forth circumspectly. He treads carefully on this tricky subject matter. Consequently, I can assure you that he is making doubly sure that what he proposes not only squares with modern science, but is a viable explanation consistent with what the Bible teaches. In fact, Josh remains very concerned that science not be given a black eye even while insisting that all 'first principles' of our understanding derive from the Bible. He proclaims that science and the Bible don't have to be mortal enemies—they can find peace in one another's company. Both seek understanding and both can glorify God while benefiting His creatures.

Of course, this goal does not constitute an easy task. Nonetheless, Josh has done as fine a job as any I can recall to open a door to an understanding of whether spiritual reality lurks within unseen dimensions of the physical universe.

Some might wonder if this quest is wise. They would ask, "Does the Bible encourage traversing this treacherous route?" I would answer them with this verse from the Wisdom of Solomon. Proverbs 25:2 teaches: "*It is* the glory of God to conceal a thing: but the honor of kings *is* to search out a matter." One thinks of the very first verse of the Bible and how the New Testament amplifies it at the outset of the Gospel of John:

In the beginning God created the heavens and the earth. *(Genesis 1:1)*

In the beginning was the Word. And the Word was with God. And the Word was God. All things came into being through Him. Without Him, nothing came into being that has come into being. (John 1:1-3).

You see, even the Apostle John had to grapple with the reality of His experience of Jesus Christ and how his framework for understanding God, the Hebrew principle of there being only one God, could be reconciled. He knew that God was one. But he also knew that Christ was Himself fully God. His gospel asserts these truths in many poetic and dramatic ways. At the very beginning, he asserts that it was in fact *Christ who had created all that exists.* If Christ was God, He also had to be the creator. If God was one, there couldn't be one God who created the universe and one equal to Him who did nothing. To express this reality and to clarify his meaning at the same time, John borrowed some words, one in particular, from a contemporary, Philo of Alexandria and from his philosophy of the LOGOS (i.e., the *Word* of God). Philo's view challenged the then popular notion of the *demiurge* of the Greeks. John would begin with Philo's logos, but further clarified what God had revealed to us through this *Logos*, whom John equated with Jesus Christ.

Unlike Philo (a Jew) and the Greek Gnostic writings (some such heretical gospels may already have been circulating), John insisted that this Logos was more than an *aeon*, an intermediary, aka the 'demiurge' that created the world (a world made of matter that the Greeks believed was inherently degraded and would ultimately spawn evil). Instead, John insisted that Jesus was *eternal* in every sense of the word—indeed He was exactly the same as God *because He was God.* To make it plainer: He was in the very beginning with God; because *He was God.* Furthermore, everything, all things, including angels and archangels (the so-called heavenly host), were made by John's *Logos*—and no other being had any part to play in this act of creation. It wasn't that God the Father made some things and Christ made others. More to the point, it wasn't that God the Father made God the Son first, and then the Son created everything else. No, John is clear: without Christ, nothing came into being at all that had ever come into being. It began with Christ, the *only begotten* of the Father. "No man hath seen God at any time; the only begotten Son, which is in the bosom of the Father, he hath declared *him*." (John 1:18) "He that believeth on him is not condemned: but he that believeth not is condemned already, because he hath not believed in the name of the only begotten Son of God." (John 3:18) We can rest assured—John was very specific about using the term 'begotten' and not 'made.' That is why the notion of the Trinity really does find its genesis in the New Testament.

True: it would take the Church another 250 years to articulate it with more precision in the various creeds it labored to create. Nevertheless, John's first century contention explained a fundamental tenet of the cosmos: the supernatural could and did give birth to the natural. There was no need for a 'half-god, half-creature' to bring the universe into being. God Himself (Christ that is, the Logos) made it in His own studio called eternity. And when it came time (literally) for God to express Himself fully, He was completely capable of becoming a part of nature (space-time) itself. He had become fully man—just like us, yet full of the glory of the Father. And we beheld Him and His glory (He presented Himself in such a way that we could know Him). Through this act of incarnation, we were able to understand Him. This proved that the natural could embrace the supernatural and the supernatural could 'interface' with the natural because God had become one of us. "And the Word was made flesh, and dwelt among us, (and we beheld his glory, the glory as of the only begotten of the Father,) full of grace and truth." (John 1:14)

So it is that the Bible teaches it is a good thing to seek to understand the nature of God and His creation. By doing so, we understand far more about God, His love for us, and why He made us the crown of His creation. The book you are about to read contributes to that priority effort. Therefore, I commend Josh Peck and his book to you in hopes that you learn from it as have I. Through it, you will assuredly come to appreciate in more depth the creation and its wonder, as well as its wonderful Creator who applied His most beautiful design and so perfectly engineered it that He might "bring many sons to glory" (Hebrews 2:10). A heavenly calling we have indeed!

S Douglas Woodward

Oklahoma City

July, 2014

Introduction

I have always been fascinated by various areas of science and Christianity. I remember, as a child brought up in a Christian home, I had an extreme hunger for discovery that would sometimes get me in trouble. When I was around ten years old, I received a chemistry set as a gift. That evening, unbeknownst to my mother, I opened the chemistry set, discarded the instructions, and decided to go at it on my own. Within ten minutes of mixing random chemicals, my mother and I were experiencing intense headaches from the fumes. Our house smelled of sulfur for days after. Needless to say, my mother was not amused.

Later on in life, I became more interested in the idea of science in the Bible. I remember learning about Matthew Fontaine Maury: an oceanographer who first discovered underwater currents by taking the Psalms of the Bible literally.[1] This was one of the first examples I had ever heard concerning someone using the Bible to initiate a scientific discovery.

It wasn't soon after that I began hearing Christian apologists and evangelicals using science to back up the claims of the Bible. I would hear this in terms of refuting evolution and trying to determine the age

---

[1] "The fowl of the air, and the fish of the sea, and whatsoever passeth through the paths of the seas." Psalm 8:8 (KJV)

of the earth. Once I learned of some of the strange claims made within the science of quantum physics, I began to wonder if the Bible contained any additional information.

That is what led me to write this book. The main idea with all of this is that science and religion do not have to be mutually exclusive. Einstein himself wrote *"science without religion is lame, religion without science is blind."* True science and true religion should be able to go hand in hand without conflict.

The problem is not that science doesn't agree with religion. The problem is certain interpretations of science don't always agree with certain interpretations of religion. At times, a scientific observation will be made and the scientist making the observation will provide the interpretation. While the actual observation reflects truth, the interpretation of the observation may not. A good example of this is Charles Darwin and his observation of life on the Galapagos Islands. While he may have accurately described what he was seeing, his interpretations did not contain the same level of truth.

This happens within religion as well. We can look at this from an honest and personal perspective. How many times have you or I thought we knew something about the Bible only to study further and discover we were wrong? Any honest person who is actively involved in objective Bible study will admit this can happen quite often. Nobody has perfect theology. While we know the Bible contains 100% truth, our interpretations of the Bible are not always as accurate. If they were, we would all agree on everything, there would be no separate denominations, and we wouldn't argue over things such as the timing of the rapture.

Throughout my life I have looked into a wide variety of sciences, but quantum physics was always the one that fascinated me most. What I hope to show in this book is, while many interpretations of quantum physics can be unbiblical and even a bit "New-Agey", we don't need to throw the entire study out. We can make the same observations and come to different conclusions that line up with the Bible. For example, just because certain physicists will state that quantum physics supports the idea of an impersonal and unconscious god or "force", that does not mean you must accept that interpretation if you choose to believe in the science of quantum physics.

The fact is, something strange is happening on a quantum level. Many individuals go to ideas of multiple universes, faster than light travel, or even extraterrestrial involvement to explain some of these things. We must keep in mind that many (not all, and possibly not even most) physicists are trying to explain these things outside of a biblical worldview without God. For example, while certain physicists and cosmologists will struggle with the idea of what caused the Big Bang, all we Christians have to do is open the Bible to the book of Genesis. This in no way should make us feel that we are better or smarter than these physicists, lest we fall into pride. Rather, it should make us realize that we are all searching for answers. Concerning things like this, we are looking at the same problem from different angles. We, as Christians, just have the extra help from the Creator of all to put things in perspective.

Throughout this book, I will take you on the same journey I embarked on in reconciling quantum physics with the Bible. This is by no means an exhaustive study, but my hope is this will provoke further study on your own. We will cover a variety of topics having to do with the science and theology of quantum physics.

We will start by describing one of the biggest problems of scientific interpretation and how it relates to Gnosticism. Then we will define the fourth spatial dimension and compare it with the dimension of time. We will see how ideas of the fourth spatial dimension helped shape science and culture over the past hundred years. We will also look at the UFO phenomena and, equipped with what we learned about the fourth spatial dimension, see how it is scientifically far more likely and logical that these craft and their pilots are coming from a place outside of our dimension rather than merely outside of our planet.

We will then look at the basic theories concerning higher dimensions above the fourth. Next, we will take a brief look into particle physics and show what composes our reality. We will then look at things like string theory, M-theory, and branes to determine if we can find any biblical basis for these fascinating ideas. After that, we are going to discover the great mysteries surrounding time and entropy. We will even talk with a physicist who may have unlocked the secret to time travel.

After all of this, we will look at the Creator Himself and some of His more obscure attributes. We will see how these attributes are embedded in the nature of quantum mechanics. Lastly, we will see how all of this applies to us as individuals and how we were created with the potential for some of the same obscure attributes as the Creator.

INTRODUCTION

I must state upfront that I am not a physicist nor a scientist of any kind. I am simply a Bible-believing Christian who has a deep appreciation for God's creation and the study of quantum physics. I have written things in this book as easy to understand as possible and have chosen to leave things out that I do not understand or am unable to adequately describe. I would also like to state that one of the most exciting things I learned in researching for this book is that these ideas are not impossible for the layman to understand. I consider myself very much a layman and was fascinated to discover there is nothing to be afraid of concerning being "sufficiently intellectual" or "smart enough" to appreciate the field of quantum physics.

It is my sincere hope that this book becomes as much a blessing for you to read as it was for me to write. I pray this will help expand your horizons as well as gain a wider appreciation for the majesty of our God and His creation. Above all else, I pray this will help you develop a closer relationship with God or, if you do not know Him, help you to be able to start one.

Thank you for reading, take care, and God bless!

Josh Peck

www.ministudyministry.com

joshpeckdisclosure@gmail.com

QUANTUM CREATION

Chapter 1

Teachings from Higher Dimensions

*But there were false prophets also among the people, even as there
shall be false teachers among you, who privily shall bring in damnable
heresies, even denying the Lord that bought them, and bring upon
themselves swift destruction.*

2 Peter 2:1 (KJV)

Why Science is often an Enemy of Theology

Quantum physics is sometimes used as support for some rather
strange theological teachings. In reality, these teachings stem
from an interpretation of science and not the science itself. We
can see this by looking at how the theology is far older than the science
of quantum physics. If the theology predates the science, then clearly
the science is not needed for the theology to exist. In short, the science
of quantum physics is not at fault for the anti-biblical teachings
sometimes attached to it. Rather, it is the fault of the scientific
interpreter.

As we will describe in more detail later, this book is written with
the understanding that the spiritual world described in the Bible and the
dimensions of space above our own are essentially the same thing. What

we will primarily deal with is not necessarily Heaven, at least not in the sense of what we typical recognize as the Kingdom of God. Rather, we will be mostly dealing with the part of spiritual creation that coincides with, and sometimes bleeds into, our own.

We are dealing with a reality that, according to the Bible, demons and fallen angels inhabit. Sometimes it is necessary for God to send one of His holy angels through this realm in order to deliver a message to a mortal man. However, such as is described in the book of Daniel, they are sometimes met with restraint from the denizens of this strange realm. As Christians, we may call this place *"the second heaven"*, *"beyond the veil"*, or quite simply the spiritual world.[2] Most new-agers might call it the *"astral plane."*[3]

Concerning this place, there is a duality and dichotomy of views between Christianity and New Age theology. Both believe in its existence; however, Christianity recognizes it as a place we are forbidden to travel whereas New Age theology celebrates traversing to higher dimensions. What we have are two separate teachings about a single spiritual environment. How do we know which teaching is true?

---

[2] The term "the second heaven" can also be used in reference to outer space, depending on the context. My good friend Douglas Hamp is the one who introduced me to the term "beyond the veil."

[3] My familiarity with New Age theology comes from personal experience when, years ago, I was involved in things such as astral projection and remote viewing. As I have stated in other books and radio interviews, I am completely against these practices now and have come to the conclusion that no good can come from participating in such activities. In my experience, all they lead to are deception, confusion, and open doors that are meant to stay closed.

For us Christians, the answer is simple: consult the Bible. However, that answer isn't always easy for everyone. Some people, Christians and non-Christians alike, have trouble with relying on only one book, or rather one collection of sixty-six books, to define their entire belief system. Many times, they will feel the Bible is not sufficient to answer all of their questions. I myself used to have this same outlook which is what led me into the dangerous world of New Age theology, perhaps more accurately known as Gnosticism. Most people normally would not equate New Age with Gnosticism, let alone say they are the same thing, but when examined, the similarities are striking.[4]

The Basics of Gnosticism

The way the spiritual world works is described quite differently in Gnosticism when compared against the Bible. Even the idea of an ultimate creator is skewed. The best place to begin with this is the story of creation itself.

In Gnosticism, the ultimate creator is more of a force than a personal being. This force is sometimes called "the true god" or "the light." Gnostics view this force as impersonal yet able to create personal gods, known as "aeons". The original impersonal force is neither male nor female, but it brings forth male and female aeons. These aeons exist in the middle realm of a three-tiered creation. Gnosticism teaches that our physical realm is the bottom tier; the top tier is where the impersonal creator force is, and the created aeons exist in the middle tier.

---

[4] For more information on this, check out *Demonic Gospels* by Dr. Ken Johnson.

Gnosticism teaches that ages ago, these male and female aeons procreated and, in a sense, produced other aeons. Gnosticism also teaches that when all these aeons are together under the true light, everything is in harmony. This is called "the fullness". It conveys the idea that the aeons are the expression of the true light; together they are the sum of the fullness of the true light.

One of these aeons is called the "logos" or "son". For us Christians, that should immediately ring a bell. In the Bible, the logos is Jesus Christ, the Son of God. However, in Gnosticism, the idea is not the same. Gnosticism teaches that the logos is the highest in the hierarchy of the aeons, and yet it is still below the true light. It was the first thing produced by the true light. It is sometimes referred to as "form of the formless", "body of the bodiless", and "face of the invisible" among other things.[5]

The lowest aeon in the hierarchy is known as "Sophia." Gnostic literature states that Sophia was so low in the hierarchy that she was actually close enough to the physical world to be able to interact with it. It is taught that Sophia rebelled against the rules of the other aeons by committing the sin of creating a being without her male aeon counterpart. Consider this passage from Gnostic literature:

---

[5] For more information on this, watch Dr. Michael Heiser's presentation entitled Introducing Gnosticism on YouTube (much of the information contained in this section can be found in both Introducing Gnosticism by Dr. Michael Heiser and Demonic Gospels by Dr. Ken Johnson).

"A thing came out of her which was imperfect and different from her appearance, because she had created it without her consort."[6]

Also consider some of the claims this "thing" makes and the interpretations the Gnostic text provides:

"For he said, 'I am God and there is no other God beside me,' for he is ignorant of his strength, the place from which he had come."

"And when he saw the creation which surrounds him, and the multitude of the angels around him which had come forth from him, he said to them, 'I am a jealous God, and there is no other God beside me.' But by announcing this he indicated to the angels who attended him that there exists another God. For if there were no other one, of whom would he be jealous?" [7]

This "thing" is known by many names in Gnosticism. It is called the *"Demiurge"* meaning the "maker." It is also called *"Yaltabaoth"* meaning "child, come forth", *"Saklas"* meaning "fool", and *"Samael"* meaning "blind one". In Gnostic literature, this being, this "thing", is actually YHWH, the God of the Bible. Clearly, Gnostic teaching has a very different, disrespectful, and even insulting view of our God.

The reason I bring this up is the fact that, at times, people teaching New Age theology and/or Gnosticism will make it seem like they believe essentially the same thing as the Bible. They will sometimes try and pair the two to make it more palatable for Christians. In reality, nothing could be further from the truth. Gnostic teaching and anything relating to it are strictly forbidden by the Bible. This, of course, is found

---

[6] Apocryphon of John, NHC – this can be read free of charge at http://www.gnosis.org/naghamm/apocjn.html
[7] Ibid.

in numerous places, but probably the best example is found in the New Testament book of 1 John:

> *2:22 Who is a liar but he that denieth that Jesus is the Christ? He is antichrist, that denieth the Father and the Son.*
>
> *23 Whosoever denieth the Son, the same hath not the Father: he that acknowledgeth the Son hath the Father also.*[8]

Gnostic teaching clearly denies the Father and the Son. The teaching of Gnosticism, according to the standards set by 1 John, would be considered as opposed to Christ (antichrist). Thus, Gnosticism and Christianity could not be farther apart in theology.

The reason Gnostics consider their version of God, also known as the Demiurge, to be a fool is because he claims he is the only God. To a Gnostic, there are many gods called aeons. Therefore, Gnostics believe they have knowledge that not even the Demiurge himself has. That is why they consider him to be ignorant, blind, and foolish. Gnostics also consider the Demiurge to be quite unreasonable and malicious because he doesn't want humanity to know the truth about these other gods.

Gnosticism teaches that the Demiurge created angels; however, the angels are called *"archons"* and never rebelled.[9] In fact, as Gnostic literature states, the archons obediently joined with the Demiurge to create Adam. That is to say, the Demiurge needed the help of the angels

---

[8] 1 John 2:22-23 (KJV)
[9] The word "archons" can be found in the Bible as well, specifically in the book of Ephesians where it talks about the fallen angels that are under Satan's rule.

to create man. Adam was created to be a slave to the Demiurge and the archons.

Sophia eventually saw what was going on and took pity on mankind. Through this, Sophia realized her mistake and a *"spark of the divine"* was put into Adam.[10] This is how Gnosticism explains Adam being flesh and spirit instead of a mindless slave. Interestingly enough, according to Gnostic texts, Adam had the spark but Eve did not. Eve is considered as less than Adam. There is no idea of equality between men and women or even "different yet equally important roles" in Gnostic literature like there is in the Bible. Gnosticism makes the clear and incredibly mistaken distinction that a woman is less than a man.

Later on, the aeons (including the Holy Spirit, Christos, and Jesus, which are all different beings in Gnosticism) decided they wanted Sophia back to once again complete the fullness that was lost. Jesus appeared to Sophia as a type of cosmic cross to try and bring her back. Sophia then is reunited with her counterpart, the cosmic Jesus, as he becomes her bridegroom.

Many of these terms probably sound very familiar. These are terms used throughout the Bible, but make no mistake; they are certainly not expressing the same ideas. It is this type of Gnostic teaching that gave birth to New Age ideas such as the cosmic Jesus and Christ consciousness. Unfortunately, many of these strange beliefs and interpretations have made their way into quantum physics. This is the

---

[10] Gnostic literature disagrees how exactly this was done. In one version, the Demiurge was tricked into doing it. In another, Sophia did it herself.

reason that background information into Gnosticism is necessary in a book such as this. It is important to show that proper spiritual and biblical discernment is needed in examining some of the claims and interpretations that modern science postulates.[11] It is also important to recognize that these deceitful interpretations should not be enough for us to throw science out altogether. Using biblical discernment, we can look at these scientific observations and interpret them without having to resort to New Age and Gnostic theology. When we have the proper interpretation of scripture and the proper interpretation of scientific observation, they should both agree in full. They both should act as two pillars holding up the true understanding of reality. If they do not agree, then one or both of the pillars are broken and must be fixed, otherwise the whole structure will come crashing down.

Opposing Views

I stated at the top of this chapter that there are two opposing views on how the spiritual world works; Gnosticism teaches one and the Bible teaches another. Of course, there are more ways to look at the spiritual world but most are an offshoot of one of these two originalities.

---

[11] For an example of this, refer to the documentary *What the Bleep Do We Know?* But be forewarned, this is not at all a Christian interpretation of modern physics and other sciences. It is filled with ideas of New Age, Gnosticism, strong language, and even blasphemy in certain parts. I will state too that not all physicists and scientists view scientific observation in these ways. I believe the ones that do are a minority at this point, but unfortunately, it is usually that minority that gets all the attention and airtime. Because of this, the minority is growing and will continue to do so. This is why we need more Christians in these fields with strong discernment to determine proper interpretations of scientific observations.

It is my opinion that if we want to know the truth about the spiritual world, we need to consult the Bible. In my humble opinion, the demonically-inspired beliefs of Gnosticism should play no part in a search for truth. One good example of why I believe in the legitimacy of the Bible over Gnostic texts is the vast amount of fulfilled prophecy in the Bible. I don't know any other being, whether physical or spiritual, that has ever written a prophetic text with 100% accuracy besides the God of the Bible. This is something Gnostic texts lack.

Interview with Dr. Ken Johnson

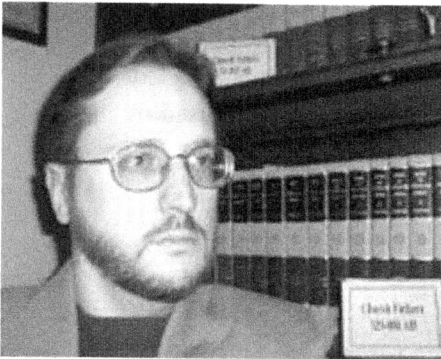

Figure 1 - Dr. Ken Johnson is the author of Demonic Gospels: The Truth about the Gnostic Gospels, Ancient Church Fathers, Ancient Prophecies Revealed, Ancient Post Flood History, and many others.

One who shares my opinions and someone who I have had the pleasure of getting to know over the course of the past few months is biblical researcher Dr. Ken Johnson (Figure 1). Ken agreed to share his insights with me on multiple occasions: twice on my podcast *The Sharpening* and also with an interview for this book. Ken has proven to be an excellent resource for information concerning many facets of Bible study.

If you wish to listen to and watch the previous interviews I conducted with Dr. Ken Johnson, you can view my YouTube channel at www.youtube.com/joshpeckdisclosure. The episodes are entitled *The Sharpening 009: Dr. Ken Johnson and the Truth about the Gnostic*

Gospels and *The Sharpening 030: Dr. Ken Johnson and Bible Prophecy Revealed.* For this book, I contacted Ken to provide his insights into this topic because it is one he, as the author of numerous books concerning ancient texts, is very well familiar with.

JOSH PECK: In what major ways do the Biblical gospels and the Gnostic gospels differ?

DR. KEN JOHNSON: The Biblical gospels teach that we are saved by what Jesus did on the cross; the Gnostic gospels teach we save ourselves by meditation and obtaining a Christ consciousness. There are extra-biblical texts the Bible recommends, like the book of Jasher and the book of Enoch. There are also the writings of the ancient Church fathers we can look at. Those texts may not be 100% accurate, but they still contain good information. However, the Gnostic gospels are never recommended or endorsed by the Bible or any other Christian text.

JOSH PECK: According to Gnostic theology, how does one attain salvation?

DR. KEN JOHNSON: Gnostic teaching states that you are saved by works and through Gnosis, a kind of meditation. You have to come to the realization that there is a piece of God inside of you and learn how to enter into your own godhood, among other things. They also consistently teach that there are seven sacraments you have to go through in order to be saved.

JOSH PECK: What in the Bible leads you to believe Gnostic teaching is a demonic doctrine?

DR. KEN JOHNSON: Paul says if anyone brings another doctrine (about Jesus and the Holy Spirit) than what we have preached to you, let them be accursed. Gnostic teaching conflicts with the Bible so much that the Bible defines it as demonic, meaning being of some other fallen source removed from God. Gnostic writings teach that the God of the Bible is demented because he doesn't realize he isn't the only one. It teaches that you are God and if you realize it, you will be saved. It is completely different than what the Bible teaches.

JOSH PECK: Is there a root of Gnosticism in the world's unbiblical religions and beliefs today, and if so, how?

DR. KEN JOHNSON: Most all of the false religions teach some form of magic with meditation in them. The way to pick them out is simple. You have the Bible that gives a plan of salvation and proves itself by fulfilled prophecy in our lifetime. If someone else comes along with absolutely no prophecy and gives a completely different method of salvation, then you know it isn't real.

JOSH PECK: Do you see Gnostic beliefs presenting themselves in other places we might not normally expect, such as in modern science, and if so, how?

DR. KEN JOHNSON: Yes. For example, universities all over the country teach evolution. We also have things like yoga classes all over (including the YMCA).

JOSH PECK: If a person believes Gnostic teaching to be true, what types of things can we say to steer them toward the right path?

DR. KEN JOHNSON: We should be able to explain to them that the Bible contains accurate prophecy fulfilled in our lifetime which proves it to be of supernatural origin. For example, there have been over fifty very specific prophecies that have been fulfilled since 1948, which was when Israel became a nation. Then we should know how to explain exactly how we came to be here by showing evolution is false and the creation story in the Bible is true. Lastly, we need to be able to explain what is needed for true salvation in the way the Bible describes it.

JOSH PECK: If people want to know more about you, your work, or order your books, where can they go?

DR. KEN JOHNSON: They can go my website, Biblefacts.org, for any information on me, my work, and ministry. They can find my books on my website and also on Amazon.com.

* * *

A very special thanks goes out to Dr. Ken Johnson for providing his expertise in this interview.

Chapter 2

Defining Five Dimensions

While we look not at the things which are seen, but at the things which are not seen: for the things which are seen are temporal; but the things which are not seen are eternal.

2 Corinthians 4:18 (KJV)

Differing Terms

The term *"fourth dimension"* can easily become confused if not properly defined. The idea of a fourth dimension can be used to explain two different things. Usually, it depends on the context in which the term is used. Before we can fully understand the two ways the term *"fourth dimension"* can be used, we must define what we mean by the word *"dimension"*.

What is a dimension? That is a question I had to ask myself early on in preparation for writing this book. Before I did much research on the topic, my idea of dimensions was defined by various science fiction television shows and movies. I had the thought that we lived in our dimension and there could exist another dimension "out there". I considered the idea that this other dimension was inhabited by a variety of exotic creatures and was located beyond the edge of the known universe. As I quickly discovered, in some ways, my preconceived notions were right. However, to my excitement and delight, many other notions I had were dead wrong.

To fully understand the idea of another dimension, I had to go back to basics. That is exactly what I will do here in order to take you along the same journey of discovery that led me to the fourth dimension. I believe it is important to begin with the most relatable example: our world.

We all live in a world of three dimension. These three dimensions are where everything we encounter every day is located. These three dimensions can best be explained with the aid of axes.

Axes can be defined as one-dimensional lines that continue on forever. We can use three perpendicular axes to plot out any point in physical space. First, we have an axis called x. The x axis is used to plot points from side to side and defines the first dimension. The next axis, defining the second dimension, is called y and is used to plot points forward and backward. Lastly, defining the third dimension, is the z axis, used to plot points up and down. We can use these three axes to plot any point in space by combining them together at the same point (Figure 2). We have even been created with an example of this. You can use you hand to show these three axes (Figure 3). Using the x, y, and z axes, all of physical existence that we can experience, from the tip of

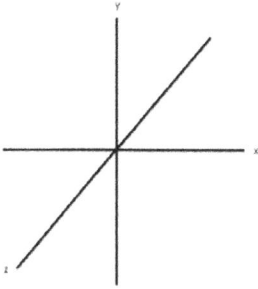

Figure 2 - The x, y, and z axes can be used to plot out any point in physical existence. The x axis defines side to side, the y axis defines forward and backward, and the z axis defines up and down.

your nose to the furthest observable star and beyond, can be conceivably located and plotted. This is what it means to live in a world of three dimensions.

There are at least two different classifications of dimensions. The three dimensions we live in are known as *"spatial dimensions"*. There is also one dimension of time. This is known as a *"temporal dimension"*. Later in this book, we will be delving into ideas surrounding time travel and even speak with a physicist who believes he may have found a way for it to be possible, but for now only the terms are important. Through these terms are where some confusion can come in. When speaking of knowable dimensions, it has been stated that we live in four dimensions (three spatial and one temporal). This is absolutely correct. When referring to a possible unknown spatial

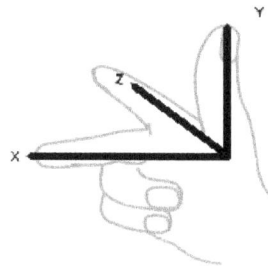

Figure 3 - We have a built-in example of the x, y, and z axes. By stretching out the middle finger, index finger, and thumb to perpendicular 90 degree angles, we can show the three dimensions that make up all of physical existence.

dimension, this too is often described as a fourth dimension, which is also absolutely correct. That is why it is always important to pay attention to the context of the discussion when references of a fourth dimension come into play.

The reason these two dimensions were originally classified as the fourth dimension will be explained later in this book. As of today, there are different tricks that people, specifically theoretical physicists, will use to better define which classification of dimension they are talking about. When referring to time as the fourth dimension, some will say *"three plus one dimensions"* whereas others will say *"three spatial and one temporal"*. When referring to a higher spatial dimension than the three we can experience, some will say *"fourth spatial dimension"*. Others will plainly call it *"the fourth dimension"* while assuming it to be understood that in an environment of four spatial dimensions, time would be the fifth dimension. If we were speaking of an environment of five spatial dimensions, time would be the sixth dimension, and so on.

Everyone who writes on this and related topics has their own way of conveying these ideas. Not everyone will explain their terminology in the beginning of their books. That is why I will state my personal use of terminology here. Throughout this book, we will mostly be focusing on five dimensions in total; four of space and one of time. When I am referring to time, I will either plainly use the word *"time"* or the term *"first temporal dimension"*. When I am referring to the next unknowable dimension of space above our own, I will refer to it as the *"fourth spatial dimension"*. My hope is this will help minimize confusion throughout this book, especially when we get into subjects that can already be a bit confusing on their own.

CHAPTER 2

There is a wide variety of other words and terms I will be using through this book that may not be familiar to every reader. When these come up, I will define them to the best of my ability to avoid any potential confusion. Now that we have the main terms concerning the fourth dimension defined, we can move on to the next phase of this journey.

Chapter 3

Visualizing the Fourth Dimension

For now we see through a glass, darkly; but then face to face: now I know in part; but then shall I know even as also I am known.

1 Corinthians 13:12 (KJV)

Reasons for Study

It is easy for us to visualize objects within our three dimensions of space. We can even visualize one and two-dimensional space. When it comes to the fourth spatial dimension, however, visualization is near to impossible. The question could then come up, why bother with a fourth spatial dimension that we can't even imagine?

I believe there are many good answers to this question. First of all, it is important because it is a part of God's creation.[12] Learning things and entertaining possibilities can help us understand the

---

[12] In modern physics, the idea of a fourth spatial dimension is theoretical. However, I equate the fourth spatial dimension with the spiritual world, so I am treating it as biblical fact.

complexities of God's design. This understanding can lead to a fuller grasp of some of the more supernatural things written about in the Bible.

Second, it can be used as an apologetic and witnessing tool. If you are attempting to defend your faith or share the gospel with someone who already has an understanding of some of the theories surrounding modern physics, it is a great advantage to be able to speak to them in terms they will understand. This is especially true in providing answers from a biblical worldview to questions that come from a scientific worldview.[13]

Third, because it's just plain fascinating! The idea of a reality beyond what we can physically experience is a belief that falls right in line with biblical Christianity. Why wouldn't we want to know more about it if we have the opportunity? Of course, there are many other reasons for this type of study. These are just the top three in my personal list.

Even though we may not be able to visualize what a fourth spatial dimension would look like, there are tricks we can use to help us understand it. We will be looking at a few of these tricks throughout this chapter. This is by no means a completely exhaustive study of all of the methods used to help explain the fourth spatial dimension. The examples

---

[13] Common examples of those who employ this tactic are Christians who study the earth sciences to defend the position of a young earth creation or Christians who study biology to refute the theory of evolution. In the same way as these, the study of modern physics can aid in defending a belief in spiritual existence.

included here are merely a few that are easier to grasp among the many that are available.

Flatland

Probably the best method I have come across in understand higher spatial dimensions is used in fictitious literature. One popular example of this among physicists, and one I will be referring to from time to time throughout this book, is a novella entitled *Flatland* (Figure 4).[14] The basic idea is to use the written word to help the reader imagine what our three-dimensional world would look like from the perspective of a two-dimensional being. When considering the two-dimensional perspective, it can help us understand what the fourth spatial dimension would look like compared to our three-dimensional world.

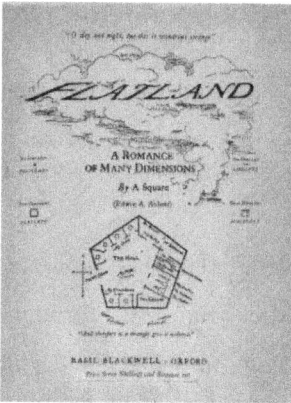

Figure 4 - Flatland cover, 6th edition

In *Flatland,* the main character, named A. Square, tells us of his experience as a two-dimensional square who later encounters the third spatial dimension. He begins his story by first explaining what his reality would look like from our three-dimensional perspective. To quote A. Square in *Flatland*:

"Nothing was visible, nor could be visible, to us, except straight Lines; and the necessity of this I will speedily demonstrate. Place a

---

[14] *Flatland: A Romance of Many Dimensions* by E.A. Abbot, 1884

penny on the middle of one of your tables in Space; and leaning over it, look down upon it. It will appear a circle. But now, drawing back to the edge of the table, gradually lower your eye (thus bringing yourself more and more into the condition of the inhabitants of Flatland), and you will find the penny becoming more and more oval to your view; and at last when you have placed your eye exactly on the edge of the table (so that you are, as it were, actually a Flatland citizen) the penny will then have ceased to appear oval at all, and will have become, so far as you can see, a straight line. "[15]

Since Flatland would only consist of the x and y axes, there would be no up or down. There would only be side to side and front to back. Because of this, the perspective of Flatlanders would be considerably different from our own. Any shape they would be looking at would appear to them as a line.

Imagine if you were able to breach Flatland as a three-dimensional being. Let's say you were able to stick your finger through their two-dimensional space. How would that look to the Flatlanders? They would see a very small line segment appear out of nowhere.[16] As your finger passes through the two-dimensional plane, they would see the line segment grow in size. When you take your finger out again, they

---

[15] Ibid. Part 1, Section 1

[16] In two-dimensional reality, this actually would be translated as a circle, but since Flatlanders lack the ability to see the entire shape, it would look to them as a line. Similarly in our three spatial dimensions of reality, we cannot see around to the backside of solid and opaque objects that are right in front of us.

would see the line segment shrink in size then disappear again, seeming to vanish in thin air (Figure 5).

If you really wanted to give the Flatlanders something to talk about, you could stick your whole hand through their two-dimensional space. They would first see a small line segment appear as the tip of your middle finger breaches the two-dimensional plane. Next, your index and ring fingers would break through. The Flatlanders would see two more segments appear at either side of the

Line segment from the perspective of two dimensions

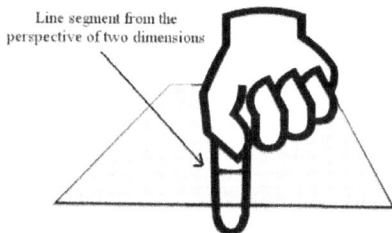

Figure 5 - From a two-dimensional perspective, the Flatlanders would only see a line segment if a finger were to breach their plane of existence.

first one as the first one grows in size. Then, as your pinky and thumb break through, they would see two more segments appear. What they see next would be truly surprising. As the rest of your hand goes through, they would see all five segments combine into one large segment. Then, as your wrist went through, they would see the large segment shrink in size. When you pull your hand out, they would see the entire spectacle again, only this time in reverse; until all of the segments disappear completely.

Now imagine if you were able to take a Flatlander out of his two-dimensional environment and thrust him into our third spatial dimension. What would he see? The Flatlander would still have eyes that could only perceive two dimensions. Even if you tried to position him in a way that was facing directly at you, all the Flatlander could see would be a line made of differently colored segments. His view of your hair, face, shirt, pants, and shoes would be nothing more than multicolored line. If you were moving, the Flatlander would only see a single line of changing color.

We can use the example of Flatland to help understand what a four-dimensional interaction would like in our three-dimensional world. If a four-dimensional sphere (often referred to as a *"hypersphere"*) were to move through our three spatial dimensions, we would only be able to perceive it through our three-dimensional eyes. We would see a very tiny sphere suddenly appear as it breaches our dimension. We would see the sphere grow in size as it moves through our dimension, shrink in size as it moves out, then disappear completely. Using the same example, if we were able to travel to the fourth spatial dimension, from our perspective, it would look like three-dimensional objects were changing color, growing, shrinking, appearing, and disappearing as they moved through four-dimensional space. These, of course, would not actually be three-dimensional objects. They would possess a fourth dimension, but since our eyes can only perceive three dimensions, to us they would look like ever-changing three-dimensional objects.

This also helps explain why we can't actually see the fourth spatial dimension. Just as Flatlanders would have no concept or method of truly perceiving the z axis that defines the third spatial dimension, we have no way of perceiving the fourth spatial dimension. In fact, German physicist Hermann von Helmholtz compared our inability to see the fourth spatial dimension to the inability of a blind person to understand color. There is no way to describe a color to someone who lacks the ability to actually see it for themselves. Another interesting thing to consider is the fact that though Flatlanders wouldn't be able to perceive the third dimension, it is all around them. In fact, it is even touching them. That is how the fourth spatial dimension is in relation to us. Though we can't even begin to picture what the fourth spatial dimension would look like, it is all around us. It is touching us. The reality of spiritual existence is here; it is literally right in front of our faces.

Another interesting idea from Flatland is that of imprisonment. In Flatland, a circle can simply be drawn around a Flatlander to imprison him in jail. For the Flatlander, escape would not be possible. However, if a three-dimensional person were to come along, pull the imprisoned Flatlander into the third spatial dimension, move him outside of the circle jail, then place him back in the two-dimensional plane, the Flatlander would be free. To other Flatlanders, it would look as though the Flatlander disappeared while in jail, then reappeared outside of it.

This might help us wrap our heads around Peter's miraculous jailbreak in the book of Acts. As it is written:

12:1 Now about that time Herod the king stretched forth his hands to vex certain of the church.

2 And he killed James the brother of John with the sword.

3 And because he saw it pleased the Jews, he proceeded further to take Peter also. (Then were the days of unleavened bread.)

4 And when he had apprehended him, he put him in prison, and delivered him to four quaternions of soldiers to keep him; intending after Easter to bring him forth to the people.

⁵ Peter therefore was kept in prison: but prayer was made without ceasing of the church unto God for him.

⁶ And when Herod would have brought him forth, the same night Peter was sleeping between two soldiers, bound with two chains: and the keepers before the door kept the prison.

⁷ And, behold, the angel of the Lord came upon him, and a light shined in the prison: and he smote Peter on the side, and raised him up, saying, Arise up quickly. And his chains fell off from his hands.

⁸ And the angel said unto him, Gird thyself, and bind on thy sandals. And so he did. And he saith unto him, Cast thy garment about thee, and follow me.

⁹ And he went out, and followed him; and wist not that it was true which was done by the angel; but thought he saw a vision.

¹⁰ When they were past the first and the second ward, they came unto the iron gate that leadeth unto the city; which opened to them of his own accord: and they went out, and passed on through one street; and forthwith the angel departed from him.

Acts 12:1-10 (KJV)

Peter's escape can be likened to the idea of a three-dimensional being helping a Flatlander escape the circle jail. In the account of Acts, we have the angel of the Lord, a higher-dimensional being. The angel helps Peter escape imprisonment by causing the chains to fall from his hands. The angel then leads Peter out of the prison. This was such a fantastic event for Peter that, as he was following the angel, he didn't even know if what he was experiencing was true or a vision. The angel and Peter then reach the iron gate that led to the city. The iron gate opens, seemingly by itself, which allows Peter to leave.

Using examples of how these things would work in Flatland helps us understand how they could be possible in our reality. We just have to think of a similar experience that could happen in a two-dimensional plane and consider how it would look if the third spatial dimension became involved. Then we just compare that experience to the idea of a fourth spatial dimension becoming involved in our three-dimensional reality. An event such as a jailbreak would be just as miraculous to a Flatlander as it is to us when a being of higher dimensions gets involved. Now, that being said, this in no way can be used to discredit or naturalize miraculous phenomena. When a miracle happens, whether from the fourth spatial dimension, higher dimensions, or completely outside of dimensional reality, it ultimately originates from God and is still an incredibly holy and blessed experience. If anything, gaining understanding of the fourth spatial dimension should help us to appreciate God, creation, and the miraculous even more.

Other Works of Fiction

Flatland isn't the only work of fiction that tackles the mind-bending subject of the fourth spatial dimension. I do believe Flatland contains the most relatable examples that we can use in our own understanding, so I will be referring to that one specifically throughout this book. However, there are other great works of fiction that should be mentioned.

H.G Wells, author of *The Time Machine* and a slew of others, wrote of the fourth spatial dimension.[17, 18] In his short story, entitled *The Plattner Story,* H.G. Wells wrote of a science teacher by the name of Gottfried Plattner (Figure 6). In the story, Plattner conducts a chemical experiment that ends up going wrong. The result is Plattner being sent into another universe. When he returns to the real world, Plattner realizes his body is not quite the same as it was before he left. His heart is now on the right side and he is now left-handed. When he is examined, the doctors discover that Plattner's entire body has been reversed. This is deduced as proof that he moved into the fourth spatial dimension and returned.

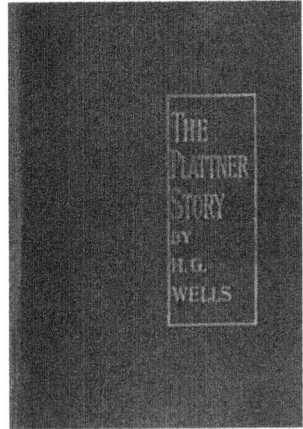

Figure 6 - The Plattner Story and Others by H.G. Wells

Of course, this type of reversal of bodily organs is not possible in our normal three dimensions of space. To understand how this could be possible with the aid of a fourth spatial dimension, we only need to think back to Flatland. If we wanted to reverse a Flatlander, all we would need to do it pull him out of two dimensions into the third, flip him around, and put him back. We might be inclined to think that all this would do to a Flatlander is cause him to be facing the opposite way, but remember, for a Flatlander, there is no up or down. Because of this, they would not have a top or bottom.

---

[17] *The Plattner Story* by H.G. Wells, Methuen & Co., London, 1897

[18] In *The Time Machine,* H.G. Wells wrote about time as the fourth dimension in a temporal sense. In *The Platter Story,* the fourth dimension he tackled was spatial.

Therefore, if one was flipped around in our third spatial dimension, when he returns to his original plane of existence, his entire body would be literally reversed.

We can use this example to understand what H.G. Wells was getting at in *The Plattner Story*. For a person's internal organs to be reversed, he would have to be "flipped around" in the fourth spatial dimension before returning. There is no way to know what exactly this would look like in four dimensions of space, but we can recognize the result of such an action. That is why it was recognized as proof that Plattner travelled to the fourth spatial dimension and returned; it would be the only way that type of body reversal could be possible. Attempting to explain what happened to Plattner in regards to the reversal he endured, the narrator of the story states…

"There is no way of taking a man and moving him about in space, as ordinary people understand space, that will result in our changing his sides. Whatever you do, his right is still his right, his left his left. You can do that with a perfectly thin and flat thing, of course. If you were to cut a figure out of paper, any figure with a right and left side, you could change its sides simply by lifting it up and turning it over. But with a solid it is different. Mathematical theorists tell us that the only way in which the right and left sides of a solid body can be changed is by taking that body clean out of space as we know it,—taking it out of ordinary existence, that is, and turning it somewhere outside space. This is a little abstruse, no doubt, but anyone with any knowledge of mathematical theory will assure the reader of its truth. To put the thing in technical language, the curious inversion of Plattner's right and left sides is proof that

he has moved out of our space into what is called the Fourth Dimension, and that he has returned again to our world."

As an interesting side-note, in the story, Plattner encounters beings in the fourth spatial dimension. These beings are known as Watchers of the Living, or just Watchers for short. They are also reminiscent of human beings in three-dimensional space, even to the point of seeming to project certain personality traits and qualities of the specific human they are connected with by way of watching. For those who are familiar with Genesis 6, the book of Enoch, and biblical descriptions of familiar spirits, these details of the Watchers in *The Plattner Story* will prove to be quite intriguing indeed.

H.G Wells wrote another story entitled *The Wonderful Visit* in which a man accidentally shoots an angel out of the sky thinking it is a bird. When the man confronts the angel, he discovers that the angel is just as surprised by the man's existence as the man is about the angel's. Part of their conversation goes as such…

"And in some incomprehensible manner I have fallen into this world of yours out of my own!" said the Angel, "into the world of my dreams, grown real."

"It is confusing," said the Vicar. "It almost makes one think there may be (ahem) Four Dimensions after all. In which case, of course," he went on hurriedly—for he loved geometrical speculations and took a certain pride in his knowledge of them—"there may be any number of three dimensional universes packed side by side, and all dimly dreaming of one another. There may be world upon world, universe upon universe. It's perfectly possible. There's nothing so

incredible as the absolutely possible. But I wonder how you came to fall out of your world into mine..."[19]

In this story, the angel inhabits the world of the fourth spatial dimension. Beings in the angel's world are no more aware of three-dimensional humans as humans are of angels. The angel and the man deduce that they live in separate worlds that overlap. Of course, we can compare some things in this story to what the Bible says about angels, but not everything. Angels do seem to exist in a plane of existence that overlaps our own, at least to a point. However, the idea that angels aren't aware of our existence can't really be backed up by the Bible. We must keep in mind with these types of stories that they are only fiction. We might be able to glean some examples to support biblical ideas from things such as this, but we should not try to build entire doctrines out of them. That being said, it still makes for a very entertaining story.

The work of H.G. Wells opened up literature to a new type of fiction. In 1895, George MacDonald mixed ideas about parallel dimensions and mysticism with Christian symbolism in his book *Lilith*. In *Lilith*, George Macdonald tells the story of Mr. Vane, a man who comes into contact with an extradimensional being named Mr. Raven. Mr. Vane travels to the other dimension by way of a mirror with Mr. Raven. It is later discovered that Mr. Raven is, in fact, the biblical Adam. Mr. Vane also encounter giants in this realm, as well as Lilith, the supposed first wife of Adam.

---

[19] *The Wonderful Visit* by H.G. Wells, London, Macmillan and Co. and New York, 1895

Again, we must keep in mind while some of these stories might be entertaining, it doesn't mean we can gain doctrine from them. The idea of Lilith as the first wife of Adam before Eve is clearly not a biblical teaching. In fact, George MacDonald himself was a Christian Universalist, meaning he believed everyone would eventually be saved and there is no eternal damnation. Though MacDonald believed this, he did write of divine judgment and earned salvation in *Lilith*. Though he wrote of some principles that are biblical, he also wrote of many that are not. Therefore, we can't use this work as an accurate portrayal of the author's beliefs.

Another work of fiction we can look at is *The Inheritors: An Extravagant Story*, written in 1901 by Joseph Conrad and Ford M. Hueffer (aka Ford Madox Ford). *The Inheritors* is a story about fourth-dimensional beings that carry out a plan to take over the Earth (Figure 7). The main character of the story, Arthur, is a journalist with high ideals in the beginning. After meeting a mysterious woman, who is a Dimensionist (a term used in the story to describe fourth-dimensional beings), Arthur compromises his ideals in order to attract the woman and become something more in life. What makes The Inheritors particularly interesting is that there are a lot of themes throughout that go hand-in-hand with the Fringe-Christian eschatology defined by certain understandings of Genesis 6, the return of the Nephilim, the alien gospel, and others.

Figure 7 - The Inheritors by Joseph Conrad and Ford M. Hueffer

By now you have probably realized the stories referenced here are from the late 1800s to early 1900s. There are many examples from that time period as well as our own I could source that display the same themes. There are two reasons I picked these specific stories from their specific time period. First, I wanted to show that even more than a hundred years ago, the fourth spatial dimension was being discussed in literature. It was not only a scientific theory. There were lay people reading about the possibilities of the fourth spatial dimension. Second, I believe these stories adequately portray the diversity of topics that were written about during that time period concerning the fourth spatial dimension. There are many others stories containing the same themes and they continue on into today.

What I aim to do in this chapter is lay a foundation for a point I will touch on later in this book. In various forms of entertainment, from books to movies to television shows, the idea of extradimensional (sometimes mistakenly labeled as extraterrestrial) beings coming into contact with humanity is everywhere and increasing. This has been going on for more than a hundred years, especially in regards to higher dimensions. Because I personally share many beliefs that surround Fringe-Christian eschatology, I believe it is possible that humanity is being prepared for something big: something that will involve higher dimensions.

Projections

Since we lack the ability to fully visualize what a fourth spatial dimension would look like, we have to rely on different tricks to help us along. We already looked at how examples in fictional literature can help us in certain areas. There are many other tricks outside of literature that can help us as well. Many times, theoretical physicists and others will demonstrate these tricks in order to help explain their position. We can use the same methods here to help show how the spiritual world can be synonymous with the fourth spatial dimension; a place that overlaps our own world of three spatial dimensions.

In her book *Warped Passages: Unraveling the Mysteries of the Universe's Hidden Dimensions*, physicist Lisa Randall provides several examples that can help us understand the fourth spatial dimension. She explains how a projection of a three-dimensional object onto a two-dimensional surface can be used as an aid toward understanding. The problem with this, as she illustrates, is there is a substantial loss of information. Consider a shadow of a rabbit standing in front of a light source (Figure 8). If the rabbit raises its arms and a leg, the shadow can appear as a human hand. Imagine this in terms of Flatland. If the Flatlanders were to see this shadow, they would believe they had a fair idea of what the true shape is, at least in terms of two-dimensional space. Yet, due to the substantial loss of information in the projection process, the reality is the shadow only merely outlines the true form of the rabbit. In three-dimensional reality, the rabbit looks nothing like

Figure 8 - In three-dimensional reality, a rabbit looks nothing like a human hand, yet in two spatial dimensions, the two are indistinguishable.

a human hand. However, due to their limited perception, the Flatlanders would have no way of knowing this.

We can also look at an example of a cube. In three-dimensional reality, a cube has a particular shape that does not change. However, if you shine a light directly above a two-dimensional plane and put a cube in between, the shadow the cube projects would only look like a square. If you tilted the cube in a certain way, the shadow would look like a hexagon. To Flatlanders, this type of thing would be extraordinary. To see a square turn into a hexagon and still be the same object would be nothing short of a miracle. However, from our perspective, it is nothing more than a simple tilt within a third spatial dimension.

In fact, to explain a cube from a two-dimensional perspective, it would be more accurate to say that the projection is a square within a square. If the shadow looks like a single square, it is only because the top square of the cube is blocking the light. Therefore, the bottom square of the cube cannot be seen. If it could, it would look like a square within a square. The only way to see the second square is to tilt the cube slightly until the edge of the bottom square is exposed to the light, resulting in a shadow that is more hexagonal in appearance. This example can help us when we think of three-dimensional projections of four-dimensional objects, such as a hypercube.

Just as a square is an example of a cube in two dimensions, a cube can be an example of a hypercube in three dimensions. A hypercube, in essence, is a cube with four spatial dimensions. Just as a three-dimensional cube would look like a square within two dimensions, a hypercube would look like a cube within a cube if projected in three spatial dimensions (Figure 9). Just as our two-dimensional example showed, if a hypercube were "tilted" in four-dimensional space, the projection would have the appearance of a cube coming out of another cube when viewed from a three-dimensional perspective.

Now imagine how a three-dimensional object would look to us if it suddenly changed appearance. This could be one way of looking at a particular Bible passage that has led to speculation within the Church throughout the years. From the Gospel of Luke:

24:13 And, behold, two of them went that same day to a village called Emmaus, which was from Jerusalem about threescore furlongs.

14 And they talked together of all these things which had happened.

15 And it came to pass, that, while they communed together and reasoned, Jesus himself drew near, and went with them.

16 But their eyes were holden that they should not know him.

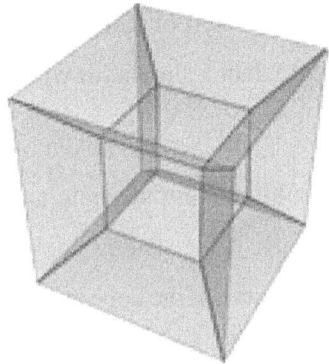

Figure 9 - A cube with four spatial dimensions is known as a "hypercube". This shows how a hypercube would be translated as a cube within a cube in three spatial dimensions. However, you would not see the inside unless it was "tilted" in four-dimensional space.

17 And he said unto them, What manner of communications are these that ye have one to another, as ye walk, and are sad?

18 And the one of them, whose name was Cleopas, answering said unto him, Art thou only a stranger in Jerusalem, and hast not known the things which are come to pass there in these days?

CHAPTER 3

¹⁹ And he said unto them, What things? And they said unto him, Concerning Jesus of Nazareth, which was a prophet mighty in deed and word before God and all the people:

²⁰ And how the chief priests and our rulers delivered him to be condemned to death, and have crucified him.

²¹ But we trusted that it had been he which should have redeemed Israel: and beside all this, to day is the third day since these things were done.

²² Yea, and certain women also of our company made us astonished, which were early at the sepulchre;

²³ And when they found not his body, they came, saying, that they had also seen a vision of angels, which said that he was alive.

²⁴ And certain of them which were with us went to the sepulchre, and found it even so as the women had said: but him they saw not.

²⁵ Then he said unto them, O fools, and slow of heart to believe all that the prophets have spoken:

²⁶ Ought not Christ to have suffered these things, and to enter into his glory?

²⁷ And beginning at Moses and all the prophets, he expounded unto them in all the scriptures the things concerning himself.

²⁸ And they drew nigh unto the village, whither they went: and he made as though he would have gone further.

²⁹ But they constrained him, saying, Abide with us: for it is toward evening, and the day is far spent. And he went in to tarry with them.

³⁰ And it came to pass, as he sat at meat with them, he took bread, and blessed it, and brake, and gave to them.

³¹ And their eyes were opened, and they knew him; and he vanished out of their sight.

Luke 24:13-31 (KJV)

Now, of course, Jesus was not a mere projection. Jesus was bodily present with these people. However, at this point, Jesus had been resurrected. Jesus had transcended the spiritual world at death and miraculously returned. Because of this, Jesus had access to capabilities that other humans did not. Jesus' resurrected body did not have the same limitations as it may have before the resurrection. That is how Jesus was able to appear different on the road to Emmaus before the eyes of the spectators were open. That is also how He was able to vanish out of their sight. While these feats are miraculous and tie right into the spiritual, we absolutely must keep in mind that Jesus was there in physical form. He was not a spirit. He was not merely a four-dimensional entity that was projecting in our three-dimensional world. Jesus came in the flesh. He demonstrated that in many ways. In the passage we just looked at, Jesus ate with those who invited Him. In understanding the idea of projections, it is important to keep in mind that this is only an example of a higher truth. Jesus was not merely a projection or a spirit; He was God in the flesh. Jesus was born on Earth as a three-dimensional human being; a form of God that humanity had the capability of understanding. After Jesus died and rose again, He had access to higher dimensions of space in His resurrected body. It is through His example that we find our hope as well. In accepting Jesus Christ as our Lord and Savior, we can be saved, be given new bodies at our resurrection, and live in eternity with God.

Unfolding

Another trick we can use to help visualize aspects of the fourth spatial dimension is by way of unfolding. In his book *Hyperspace: A Scientific Odyssey through Parallel Universes, Time Warps, and the 10th Dimension*, physicist Michio Kaku gives an example of a way to explain a three-dimensional object in two-dimensional understanding. He shows how you can unfold a cube into a two-dimensional shape (Figure 10). Interestingly enough, this shape is that of a cross. The idea is, since a cube is essentially six two-dimensional planes folded together in three-dimensional

Figure 10 - By unfolding, you can produce an object that can translate a cube into two dimensions of space.

space, you can unfold the cube to show what it would look like in two dimensions. While this idea of unfolding does not result in quite as much information-loss as a projection, it is still not a perfect device. Since there is no perfect device, if you wanted to explain a cube to Flatlanders, this is one of the methods you could use.

We can think of this in terms of three and four spatial dimensions. If we want to try and understand a hypercube, we can, in a sense, "unfold" the hypercube into three spatial dimensions. The result is what is known as a *"tesseract"* (Figure 11). Just as a cube is made of six squares, a tesseract is made of eight cubes. Though this is not a perfect device to aid in visualizing a hypercube, it can at least translate a hypercube into dimensions we can perceive.

What is also interesting about a tesseract is that it would not unfold at one-dimensional hinges like a cube does. There is a digression of dimensions when unfolding into lower dimensions. To unfold a three-dimensional cube into two-dimensional space, it must be unfolded along one-dimensional hinges (or lines).

Figure 11 - A tesseract is a hypercube that is unfolded into three spatial dimensions.

Similarly, to unfold a four-dimensional hypercube into three-dimensional space, it must be unfolded along two-dimensional planes (Figure 12).

Imagine what it would look like to a Flatlander if you were to fold the two-dimensional cross back up into a cube. From the perspective of the Flatlander, he would only see the

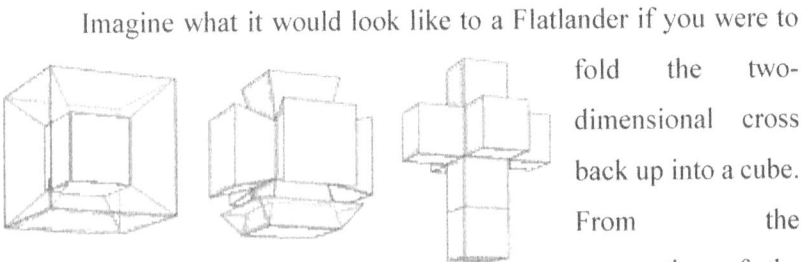

Figure 12 - In order to unfold a hypercube into three-dimensional space, it would have to be unfolded along two-dimensional planes.

two-dimensional squares disappear as they are folded up into the third spatial dimension. Similarly, if a tesseract were to be folded back up into a hypercube, we would only see the cubes disappear as they are folded up into the fourth spatial dimension.

Now imagine what would happen if the Flatlander were inside the two-dimensional cross as it is being folded up into the third dimension. Since the Flatlander has no concept of the third spatial dimension, the Flatlander would not notice anything unusual at first. He would move along the squares just as he did before the folding happened. As he moves from square to square, however, he would soon realize the squares are repeating. Upon realizing this, he would make the discovery that he is trapped. Another interesting hypothetical situation would be if the Flatlander entered the cube after it was folded up. From his perspective, the cube would look only like a common square. Upon entering, however, he would realize the inside appears much larger than the outside and there are multiple squares. Upon moving from square to square, it would be easy for the Flatlander to become confused and trapped within the cube.

We can think of this consequence of being trapped in terms of a hypercube. This is exactly the consequence Robert Heinlein explored in his short story *"...And He Built a Crooked House..."* first published in 1941. In the story, architect Quintus Teal builds a house in the shape of a tesseract.[20] He convinces his friends, Mr. and Mrs. Bailey, to purchase the house. In explaining the shape of the house, Teal gives this short explanation of the fourth dimension...

---

[20] Interestingly enough, in the story, the tesseract-shaped house is inverted, giving the appearance on an upside-down cross.

"Sure. Sure. Time is a fourth dimension, but I'm thinking about a fourth spatial dimension, like length, breadth, and thickness. For economy of materials and convenience of arrangement you couldn't beat it. To say nothing of the saving of ground space—you could put an eight-room house on the land now occupied by a one-room house. Like a tesseract—"

"What's a tesseract?"

"Didn't you go to school? A tesseract is a hypercube, a square figure with four dimensions to it, like a cube has three, and a square has two..."[21]

Before Teal gets a chance to show the Baileys the house he built, the area of Los Angeles that the house was built in suffers an earthquake. Teal and the Baileys go to inspect the house, but discover only one of the eight cubes is left standing. The other seven have mysteriously disappeared and are speculated as being stolen.

Upon entering the house, they find something quite remarkable. They discover that the other seven rooms are actually present and intact from a vantage point of within the house. They also discover the stairs of the house form a loop; the stairway in the top room lead back to the bottom room instead of leading to the roof. It doesn't take long for them to realize they are now trapped inside the house because every room just leads to another room. At one point in the story, they look down a hallway and see their own backs in front of them. These shocking

---

[21] *...And He Built a Crooked House...*, by Robert A. Heinlein, 1941

discoveries lead Teal to realize that the earthquake caused the tesseract to fold into a four-dimensional hypercube.

Teal tries to move between rooms by way of a window. He goes through the window and lands outside. Through this, he figures out that they can leave the house; it just all depends on their state of mind as they do so. Teal then reenters the house to find the Baileys.

As they continue exploring, the group realizes the windows in the top cube aren't connected as was expected. One windows leads to a view above a skyscraper, one leads to a view of an upside down expanse of water, one leads to a desert scene, and the other leads to absolute nothingness: no space, no color, not even black. They open the window that leads to the desert as another earthquake hits. They jump out of the window and find themselves in the desert. They discover from a passing truck driver that they are in Joshua Tree National Monument and, luckily, not another planet. When they return to the house, they discover the house has completely disappeared. Then Teal, in a slightly comical fashion, explains what he believes happened to the house…

"It must be that on that last shock it simply fell through into another section of space", Teal remarks. "I can see now that I should have anchored it at the foundations."[22]

Artistic Examples

Along with literary examples, analogy, and descriptive illustrations, there have also been many artists throughout time who

---

[22] Ibid.

have tried to capture ideas about the fourth spatial dimension in their art. We can use these artistic examples to try and follow the artists' line of thinking in understanding and representing this visually impossible subject. This can help us delve deeper in attempting to understand the fourth spatial dimension for ourselves.

One of the most famous attempts to artistically display the fourth spatial dimension is Salvador Dali's *Christus Hypercubus* (Figure 13). In *Christus Hypercubus* (sometimes called *Corpus Hypercubus* or *Crucifixion)*, Dali portrays Jesus Christ as being crucified on a tesseract. This oil painting can be looked at as a visual representation of how the crucifixion was a manifestation of Jesus transcending all dimensionality in time and space. According to Wikipedia...

Figure 13 - Christus Hypercubus by Salvador Dali (The Metropolitan Museum of Art. Gift of Chester Dale, Collection. 1955. © 1993. Ars, New York/Demart Pro Arte, Geneva)

"In his 1951 essay "Mystical Manifesto", he [Dali] introduced an art theory he called "nuclear mysticism" that combined Dali's interests in Catholicism, mathematics, science, and Catalan culture in an

effort to reestablish Classical values and techniques, which he extensively utilizes in Corpus Hypercubus."[23]

Of course, in the painting, the hypercube is unfolded into a three-dimensional tesseract, but the idea of the fourth spatial dimension is still expressed quite well.

Another example we can look at is *Portrait of Dora Maar* by Picasso (Figure 14). This was painted with the idea of a fourth-dimensional view, meaning the woman in the portrait could be viewed from multiple angles at once. To compare, remember what a square looks like to a Flatlander. In Flatland, to a Flatlander, a square would just look like a line. However, as three-dimensional beings with a higher perspective, we can see all the lines that make up a square at once. To us, a square looks like a square. Holding to that example, imagine what a three-dimensional object would look like to a four-

Figure 14 - Portrait of Dora Maar by Picasso (Giraudon/Art Resource. © 1993. Ars, New York/Spadem, Paris)

dimensional being. Just as we can see all the lines of a square at once, a four-dimensional being would have such clarity that they would be able

---

[23] http://en.wikipedia.org/wiki/Crucifixion_(Corpus_Hypercubus)

to see all of the six two-dimensional planes that make up a cube at once. From our perspective, this would seem confusing and garbled. This is only because we do not possess a four-dimensional perspective. To a four-dimensional being, this view of a cube would look even clearer and more complete than how we would view a cube. This is the idea being represented in *Portrait of Dora Maar*.

There are even examples in medieval art that show the attempt to convey three-dimensional information on a two-dimensional surface. They did this, in a way, by flattening space. In a floor mosaic found in an early Byzantine church, we see there is a city depicted (Figure 15). Due to the flattening of the image, there isn't much of a feel of three-dimensional perspective found in this mosaic. The artists of these types of images felt they had to project the third dimension into the second.

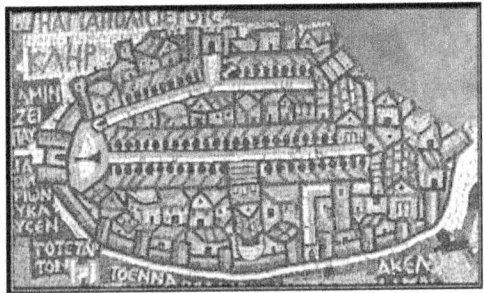

Figure 15 - Floor mosaic, early Byzantine Church of Saint George at Madaba, Jordan

We can think of this in terms of the projections and shadows we discussed earlier in this chapter. This mosaic, by itself, tells us nothing of the third spatial dimension. We see something similar in Figure 16.

All of the examples we looked at show that people all throughout time, especially within the past hundred years, have been trying to visualize and depict things that cannot be seen. The Bible is

Figure 16 - This scene, in the Bayeux Tapestry, shows English troops pointing to Halley's Comet. Just as is found in much artwork from this time period, the image lacks three-dimensional perspective. This was done deliberately to show God's omnipotence.

full of examples of attempts to explain things that are outside of our understanding. Since that time, other people have tried through literary fiction, artwork, lower-dimensional examples, and analogy to adequately represent the invisible and unknowable. The latest examples of this are found within theoretical physicists' explanations of higher spatial dimensions. We all seem to have something in us telling us there is something more to reality than what can be seen. We may not be able to fully visualize the unseen in our minds, but we can use these examples to help broaden our scope of understanding.

QUANTUM CREATION

Chapter 4

A Brief History of Fourth Dimension Beliefs

My people are destroyed for lack of knowledge: because thou hast
rejected knowledge, I will also reject thee…

Hosea 4:6 (KJV)

The Mysterious Mr. Slade

Throughout this book, we are recognizing the fourth spatial dimension as synonymous with the spiritual world through a biblical Christian worldview. There have been those, however, who have tried to equate the fourth spatial dimension with the spiritual world outside of a biblical worldview. It is important to recognize this fact and see what some of their teachings have been so we know what to avoid. Of course, many popular physicists and scientists who study higher dimensions do so outside of a biblical worldview. However, I am not only talking about them. In fact, in the grand scheme of things, I believe they are doing less spiritual damage than many others out there.[24] We must remember that we do have an enemy who takes everything of God's and attempts to twist them toward his own end.

One of the most extreme examples of this happened in the form of a trial in 1877. London newspapers popularized the claims of a man by the name of Henry Slade. These claims were so controversial and extraordinary, yet contained enough of a grain of truth, that some of the most prominent physicists of the day attended the trial. It was the publicity of this trial that made ideas of the fourth spatial dimension available outside of scientific studies. For the first time, lay people were talking about the fourth spatial dimension.

Henry Slade, born in 1835, was a self-proclaimed psychic from America. He would travel to London in order to hold séances with the townspeople. Slade was most well-known for what was known as slate-writing. During a séance, Slade would place a small chalkboard and piece of chalk under a table and claim spirits would write a message. In reality, Slade would use a variety of means to produce the writing on the chalkboard, such

Figure 17 - Depiction of one of Slade's fraudulent slate-writing methods.

---

[24] I am not completely letting atheistic science off the hook here. Any worldview that completely takes God out of the picture is harmful to the Church and causes doubt in believers; current and potential. My main point is that there are others of a more spiritual, yet unchristian and unbiblical, mindset that could pose a greater threat than we might expect.

as using his foot to write under the table (Figure 17).

Slade was caught in the act of deception multiple times.[25] During one of those times, he was arrested for fraud and charged with *"using subtle crafts and devices, by palmistry and otherwise,"* to deceive clients.[26] The trial would not have gained so much publicity had it not been for the prominent physicists who came to Slade's defense. These were not just ordinary British scientists. These were some of the greatest physicists in the world, many of whom went on to win the Nobel Prize in physics.[27]

These physicists came to Slade's aid under the assumption that some of his claims could be possible when thought of in terms of the fourth spatial dimension. The one who championed this effort was Johann Zollner; a professor of physics and astronomy at the University of Leipzig. Zollner was the one responsible for gathering together all the other leading physicists to come to Slade's defense. Among those were physicists who participated in the Society for Psychical Research and some of the most recognized and distinguished within nineteenth-century physics.

Four of the most prominent in this gathering were J.J. Thompson, Lord Rayleigh, Wilhelm Weber, and William Crooks. J.J. Thompson won the Nobel Prize in 1906 for discovering the electron.

---

[25] http://en.wikipedia.org/wiki/Henry_Slade
[26] *Fourth Dimension and Non-Euclidian Geometry in Modern Art,* Henderson, page 22.
[27] *Hyperspace: A Scientific Odyssey through Parallel Universes, Time Warps, and the 10th Dimension* by Michio Kaku, page 49.

Lord Rayleigh won the Nobel Prize in physics in 1904 and is considered one of the greatest classical physicists of the late nineteenth century. Wilhelm Weber, along with Carl Gauss, invented the first electromagnetic telegraph and even had the international unit of magnetism named after him.[28] William Crookes invented the cathode ray tube, which has been used in television sets and computer monitors.

Interestingly enough, Crookes believed it was the duty of science to study phenomena associated with spiritualism. It was actually Crookes who first influenced Zollner in the area of spiritualism. Zollner, looking for a physical and scientific explanation for spiritualism, visited Crookes at his England laboratory in 1875. It was through his visit that Zollner came to the conclusion that physics of a four-dimensional space might be the explanation for spiritualism. It was due to this belief that Zollner attempted to prove spirits as four-dimensional by conducting experiments with Henry Slade.[29]

Slade insisted he could prove his own innocence by performing his feats in front of a scientific body. Zollner, already intrigued by spiritualism, decided to take Slade up on his offer. In 1877, Zollner conducted a number of controlled experiments to test Slade's ability of sending objects through the fourth spatial dimension. Zollner invited several distinguished scientists to evaluate Slade's abilities.

---

[28] The international unit of magnetism is known as a "weber".

[29] Zollner published the content and findings of these experiments in a book titled *Transcendental Physics* in 1878.

In one experiment, Zollner gave Slade two solid rings made of wood. The idea was to test if Slade could link the two rings without breaking either one. If Slade was able to move objects through the fourth spatial dimension, this experiment would have shown it.

An example of this would be to think of two- dimensional rings in Flatland. If a Flatlander was able to manipulate the third spatial dimension, he could simply move one ring and slide it over the other, thus linking them together. The same idea applies to the fourth spatial dimension in regards to three dimensional rings. If Slade could manipulate the fourth spatial dimension, he should have been able to link the wooden rings without breaking them.

In another experiment, Slade was given the shell of a sea snail. This was to test if he could twist the coil in the shell from right-handed into left-handed. An example of this is what we discussed earlier on about Flatlanders being "flipped around" in the third spatial dimension. Another example is "The Plattner Story". If Slade was able to "flip" things around in the fourth spatial dimension, he should have been able to change around the coils of the sea snail's shell.

In yet another experiment, Slade was given a closed loop of rope. The idea was to make a knot in the circular rope without cutting it. Again, if he had access to the fourth spatial dimension, this should have been no problem.

Slade was also tested with variations of these experiments. In one variation, a rope was tied into a right-handed knot. The ends of the rope were then sealed with wax and impressed with Zollner's personal seal. Slade was asked to untie the knot without breaking the seal and retie it into a left-handed knot. In another variation, Slade was asked to remove the contents of a sealed bottle without breaking it. Just as removing a Flatlander from jail is as simple as lifting him through the third spatial dimension, Slade should have been able to remove an object from a sealed bottle by "lifting" it through the fourth spatial dimension.

Whether Slade was really able to manipulate the fourth spatial dimension is speculative. Zollner published his claims, which seemed to indicate Slade's success in showcasing his abilities, in both the *Quarterly Journal of Science* and his book *Transcendental Physics*. Zollner claimed that Slade's feats were miraculous and amazed the audience of distinguished scientists. However, it should also be stated that Slade was unable to perform some of the tests that were conducted under controlled conditions.

Zollner defended Slade and his apparent abilities, as did Weber, Crookes, and other reputable scientists. However, there were many skeptics as well. Skeptics and detractors would regard Slade as nothing more than a magician; performing illusions and sleight of hand that would not be detected by an untrained eye. It was stated that scientists would be the worst possible people to evaluate a magician because they are trained to trust their senses. Magicians are trained to bypass the senses to trick spectators and confuse reality. It was said that only another magician would be qualified to evaluate Slade's claims objectively. However, no such person observed Slade's feats under controlled conditions in the way the scientists did. When it comes to the case of Slade, we have two sides of one story and the readers are left to draw their own conclusions.

CHAPTER 4

Lenin and the Fourth Dimension

What could Vladimir Lenin possibly have to do with beliefs about the fourth spatial dimension? As it turns out, quite a bit. It is an often overlooked piece of history.

It begins with the writings of the mystic P.D. Ouspensky, who is thought responsible for introducing Czarist Russia to the idea of the fourth spatial dimension. Ouspensky wrote a number of influential books, including *The Fourth Dimension* in 1909 and *Tertium Organum* in 1912.[30] Ouspensky's writings were so influential that Fyodor Dostoyevsky explored ideas of higher dimensions and non-Euclidean geometries. He did so in *The Brothers Karamazov* through a discussion that the protagonist, Ivan Karamazov, was involved in concerning the existence of God.

Interestingly enough, the fourth spatial dimension was to play a role in the Bolshevik Revolution. Vladimir Lenin actually joined in the debate of the fourth dimension. This resulted in an influence over the science of the former Soviet Union for the next 70 years. For example, Lenin's *Materialism and Empiro-Criticism* contained his famous phrase *"the inexhaustibility of the electron"*. This phrase signified that as we look deeper into a matter, we find new layers. For example, a galaxy is

---

[30] *Tertium Organum* was especially influential to Claude Bragdon; an architect who could read Russian and was interested in the fourth dimension. Nicholas Bessarabof gave Bragdon a copy of *Tertium Organum* that was written in Russian. Bragdon then translated the text to English and incorporated his own design of the hypercube into the Rochester Chamber of Commerce building. Bragdon also published the book, which was such a success that it was taken up by Alfred A. Knopf, the New York publishing house.

made up of smaller star systems. As we look deeper, we find these systems are made of planets. If we continue probing deeper, we find that the planets are made of substances such as rock, various gases, and sometimes water. Those substances are made of molecules, which are made of atoms, which contain electrons, which, in turn, are "inexhaustible". It is also interesting to note that Russian physicists have contributed greatly in developing modern ten-dimensional theory.

After the 1905 revolution, a faction called the Otzovists developed within the Bolshevik party. By 1905, the Bolsheviks (founded by Vladimir Lenin and Alexander Bogdanov) were a major organization of workers who were governed by the principle of democratic centralism. They considered themselves to be the leaders of the revolutionary working class of Russia. The Otzovists, or *"God-builders"*, argued that the peasants were not prepared for socialism. They proposed that the Bolsheviks should use ideas and teachings of spiritualism to get the peasants used to the idea. The God-builders even quoted from Ernst Mach, a German physicist who wrote about the fourth dimension as well as the recent discovery of radioactivity.

Radioactivity was discovered by Henri Becquerel, a French scientist, in 1896. Also in 1896, radium was discovered by Marie Curie. The idea that matter could disintegrate and energy could reappear as radiation had started a major philosophical debate in French and German literary groups. The God-builders pointed this out to help build their case.

Just before this time, matter was thought to be eternal and immutable, which is a notion that came from the Greeks. The discovery of radioactivity, however, turned that idea completely around. In a sense, the foundation of Newtonian physics seemed to be disintegrating (pun reluctantly intended). Some put their faith in Mach to sort all of this out. However, Mach rejected materialism and stated that time and space were only products of our sensations. He even went as far as to write *"I hope that nobody will defend ghost-stories with the help of what I have said and written on this subject"*.[31]

By this time, a divide had developed within the Bolsheviks. This left their leader, Vladimir Lenin, questioning if ghosts and demons were compatible with socialism. In response to the mysticism and metaphysics that were becoming more popular as time went on, Lenin wrote *Materialism and Empiro-Criticism* to defend dialectical materialism. Lenin argued that the disappearance of energy and matter showed that a new dialect was emerging and did not prove the existence of spirits. He stated that this new dialect would embrace both matter and energy as two poles of a dialectal unity. Energy and matter could no longer be seen as separate, as Newton had done. Interestingly enough, three years earlier in 1905, Albert Einstein had proposed the new conservative principal that Lenin was calling out for. Of course, Lenin was not aware of this fact.

Lenin also criticized Mach's views and beliefs concerning the fourth dimension. At first he seemed to be accepting of Mach's view, stating he *"has raised the very important and useful question of a space*

---

[31] Vladimir Lenin, *Materialism and Empiro-Criticism,* in Karl Marx, Friedrich Engels, and Vladimir Lenin, *On Dialectical Materialism* (Moscow: Progress, 1977), 306-306.

of n *dimensions as a conceivable space"*, only to later point out Mach had not revealed enough about the insufficiency of observable science. Lenin criticized Mach's views because only three dimensions of space could be verified through scientific experiments. He admitted that mathematics could explore the fourth dimension but, as Lenin wrote, *"the Czar can be overthrown only in the third dimension!"*[32]

Ideas surrounding the fourth dimension and radiation proved to be quite problematic to Lenin. It took years to remove the God-builders from the Bolsheviks. Lenin succeeded, however, shortly before the outbreak of the 1917 October Revolution.

The Checkered Past of the Tesseract

As useful and integral as it is in understanding the fourth spatial dimension, the tesseract has some rather unseemly origins. This journey into history begins with Charles Hinton, who was working at the United States Patent Office in Washington, D.C. in 1905 (Figure 18).[33] Hinton was dedicated, possibly even obsessed, with visualizing the fourth spatial dimension. He also contributed to making

Figure 18 - Charles Howard Hinton

---

[32] Ibid.

[33] It was at this same time that Albert Einstein was working at the Swiss patent office and discovering the laws of relativity. Though they more than likely never met, the paths of Einstein and Hinton would later cross in interesting ways.

the effort popular. He would be known as the man who "saw" the fourth dimension.

Charles Hinton was the son of a renowned ear surgeon by the name of James Hinton. Throughout the years of his life, James Hinton became a spiritual philosopher. He promulgated beliefs of free love and open polygamy. He even became the leader of a loyal, influential, and free-thinking cult. His most famous quote was the blasphemous and insensitive remark *"Christ was the Savior of men, but I am the savior of women, and I don't envy Him a bit!"*[34]

Contrary to his upbringing, James Hinton's son Charles led a life as a mathematician. He graduated from Oxford in 1877 and became a master at the Uppingham School while working on his master's degree in mathematics. It was during his time at Oxford that Charles Hinton became intrigued with trying to visualize the fourth spatial dimension. His mathematician mind told him he could not visualize a four-dimensional object in its entirety, so Hinton developed a way to work around his human limitations. He realized it would be possible to visualize a cross section or an unfolding of a four-dimensional object. Hinton published his ideas in the *Dublin University Magazine* and the *Cheltenham Ladies' College Magazine* under the title *"What is the Fourth Dimension?"* which was reprinted in 1884 with the subtitle *"Ghosts Explained".*

---

[34] Quoted in Rucker, *Fourth Dimension,* 64.

In 1885, Hinton's upbringing seemed to catch up with him as he was arrested for bigamy and put on trial. Hinton was married to Mary Everest Boole, widow of mathematician and founder of Boolean algebra, George Boole. However, Hinton was also the father of twins born to Maude Weldon. Before being arrested, the headmaster at Uppingham had assumed that Maude was his sister. The headmaster had seen Hinton in the presence of both women and, knowing Mary to be Hinton's wife, assuming Maude to be his sister was reasonable. Hinton may have never been discovered had he not made the mistake of marrying Maude as well. When the headmaster found out Hinton was a bigamist, it initiated a great scandal. Hinton was fired, put on trial for bigamy, and imprisoned for three days. Mary Hinton decided against pressing charges and, with Charles Hinton, left England for the United States.

Hinton was then hired as an instructor of mathematics at Princeton University where he invented the baseball machine. The Princeton baseball team was able to benefit from Hinton's invention as it could shoot out baseballs at 70 miles per hour. This was the first design of baseball machines that are often used today.

After working at Princeton, Hinton accepted a job at the United States Naval Observatory. He was able to obtain the job from the influence of the observatory's director, who happened to be an advocate of the fourth spatial dimension. Then, in 1902, Hinton took a job at the Patent Office in Washington.

Hinton dedicated the rest of his life to coming up with methods by which average people could visualize the fourth spatial dimension.

CHAPTER 4

Hinton came up with an interesting concept: a type of cube that if someone tried hard enough, they could imagine the structure of a hypercube.[35] These would eventually be known and referred to as *"Hinton's Cubes"*. Hinton even came up with the name *"tesseract"* to refer to an unfolded hypercube. He also came up with the terms *"ana"* and *"kata"* to refer to the two new directions that were possible in the fourth spatial dimension.[36]

Strangely enough, Hinton's cubes became objects of mystical importance. They were used in séances and other occult practices. It was believed that by concentrating and meditating on Hinton's cubes, one could see the fourth spatial dimension which was believed to be the residence of ghosts, guides, and other spiritual entities. These occultists would spend hours in meditation, trying to mentally rearrange the cubes through the fourth dimension into a hypercube. The occultists claimed that those who could do this would experience the highest form of nirvana.

Hinton has been quite influential in scientific and occult circles. For example, Hinton influenced the thinking of previously mentioned P. D. Ouspensky. Many of the ideas Ouspensky presented in *Tertium Organum* mentioned Hinton and his ideas. Apparently, Hinton also

---

[35] A hypercube is a four-dimensional cube.

[36] With every increase of an additional spatial dimension, two new directions are required. For example, the first dimension consists of left and right. For a second dimension to be possible, the two new directions of forward and backward must be added. For the third dimension, up and down are added. Hinton realized this and gave the names of ana and kata to the two new directions required by moving up to the fourth spatial dimension.

influenced the occultist Aleister Crowley. Hinton is mentioned twice in *Moonchild,* a novel by Aleister Crowley.

Observation vs. Interpretation

In looking at these historical examples, we can get a feel for what can happen when scientific theories and discoveries are taken too far. This is why I believe it is important for the Church to have at least a base understanding of these things. We should not want scientists nor physicists, whether involved in the occult, atheism, or anything else apart from biblical Christianity, to define our doctrines for us. However, we also should not want to run from their scientific findings altogether. We have to be able to separate an unbiased scientific observation from a biased interpretation of said observation. In short, we should not want to follow Darwin and let a biased interpretation of scientific observation dictate how we believe, but we also should not want to follow Rome and imprison Galileo for proposing something scientifically unbiased just because it's different than what we are traditionally used to. There is a fine line to walk between ignorance and fear, yet if we do not fall into the extremes of either side, the journey can be an exciting, enlightening, and enjoyable one.

Chapter 5

Denizens of the Fourth Dimension

And the angels which kept not their first estate, but left their own habitation, he hath reserved in everlasting chains under darkness unto the judgment of the great day.

Jude 1:6 (KJV)

Brief Overview of the Basics

In the first chapter, we talked about some of the teachings that come from higher dimensions. Here, we are going to discuss who exactly are teaching these things. We have discussed the fourth spatial dimension as a place that is coexisting with our physical reality. Now we will discuss who exactly exists there as well as what their intentions seem to be.

When we read passages such as Genesis 6 and the book of Jude, we learn that there was a group of angels who decided to rebel against God. The cost of this rebellion was their "habitation", according to

Jude.[37] It is my belief this habitation was, in fact, the full-angelic body. I say full-angelic because it would seem angels have access to a type of physical body while also being spiritual in nature. This physical-angelic body can eat (Genesis 18:2-8), wrestle (Genesis 32:22-31), blind people (Genesis 19:11), offer protection (Psalm 91:11-12), and give visions (Daniel 10:1-12). Angels seem to have access to these bodies to be able to operate within our physical three-dimensional existence.

Since this seems to be the natural state of God's angels, to be able to operate both in Heaven and on Earth, it is reasonable to assume fallen angels had the same capabilities before they rebelled against God. However, as Jude tells us, they gave up their own habitation. It is possible that this is referring to their full-angelic (physical and spiritual) body and since they fell, they have been confined to their physical-angelic body. Of course, Jude tells us that these angels are locked in everlasting chains until the judgment. Does this mean every angel who fell is in everlasting chains? I don't believe that is what the text implies. When we read it thoroughly, it seems to indicate only those who committed the sin of human copulation as described in Genesis 6 were sentenced to everlasting chains.[38]

Notice too that Jude says they left their estate. This, in my humble opinion, is talking about Heaven and the heavenly hosts. We

---

[37] The word *"habitation"* in Jude 1:6 could very well be referring to their angelic bodies. The word in the Greek is *"oikētērion"* and could be referring to an actual dwelling, or more likely here, a dwelling for the soul: a body.

[38] I will not get too deep into this here because I have already written extensively on this topic. If you wish to learn more, refer to my book *Disclosure: Unveiling Our Role in the Secret War of the Ancients.*

also read in Revelation that Satan and his angels are cast to the Earth.[39] This gives us an in-between to deal with. The fallen angels fell from their first estate meaning they are no longer residents of Heaven. We also know they will be cast to the Earth someday, meaning they are not confined here now. So where are they?

This is a question that bears some level of speculation. It is my belief that the fallen angels reside in what I have been calling the fourth spatial dimension, and quite possibly even higher dimensions than that. If in higher dimensions, I believe this could have to do with their rank as described in Ephesians 6.[40] It could also be that they are trapped in the second heaven; a place that seems to be synonymous with outer space. Most likely, we have a duality: two different ways of looking at the same problem with two correct answers. The Bible seems to indicate that the second heaven is in reference to outer space (Deuteronomy 17:3; Jeremiah 8:2; Matthew 24:29) yet demons and fallen angels don't seem to be purely physical and three-dimensional when considering just about every description of them throughout the Bible.[41] This leads me to believe they still have access to higher dimensions and yet remain in an area above Earth when not interacting with us or our physical reality.

---

[39] Whether or not the fallen angels can still visit Heaven is another issue altogether. The main point here is simply they are not *from* there anymore; they are no longer residents of Heaven in the way the obedient angels are.

[40] For more information on this, refer to my book *Spiritual Warfare against the Satanic Government* at www.ministudyministry.com.

[41] I say "demons *and* fallen angels" because I do believe the two are different beings altogether, however this is speculative. For more information on this, refer to my book *Disclosure*.

Prepared to Provide an Answer

There is a commonly-held belief within the Church that fallen angels and demons are responsible for the so-called UFO phenomena of our day. Most churches stop there. A few go even further to explain how Genesis 6, Jude, and parts of Revelation fit in.[42] When we look at Christians and non-Christians as a whole, it would seem the majority believe UFOs are caused by something physical, such as extraterrestrial life, rather than something spiritual. For the non-Christian, there is no theological problem with this. However, this presents a problem for the Christian: if extraterrestrials exist, where are they in the Bible and how do we deal with them?

I believe most people reading this book will have a fair grasp on how to handle this problem biblically. As stated earlier, most would point to Genesis 6 to start, explain the similarities between angels and supposed extraterrestrials, and show how they could very well be the same thing. This could have some impact on an open-minded Christian, and perhaps an extremely open-minded non-Christian, but what about the rest? The majority of non-Christians aren't going to view the Bible as an authoritative source of truth, so what are we to do?

The answer is to meet them on their own terms. We need to find out what is authoritative to them. More often than not, it will be something logical. We can use scientific language with a little bit of common sense to get the same message across.

---

[42] I deal with this more in *Disclosure,* however here I am assuming most who read this book will be at least somewhat familiar with this view.

CHAPTER 5

Before getting to heavy in showing how to go about doing that, we should define a few terms. Probably everyone reading this is at least familiar with the terms *"extraterrestrial"* and *"interplanetary"*. But just to be safe, we should look at the dictionary definition of each.

extraterrestrial:

adjective

outside, or originating outside, the limits of the earth.

noun

an extraterrestrial being: a science fiction novel about extraterrestrials conquering the earth.[43]

interplanetary:

adjective

being or occurring between the planets or between a planet and the sun.[44]

For our purposes here and to make things simple, we can recognize the prefix "extra" signifies where something is from whereas the prefix "inter" signifies capabilities. For example, an extraterrestrial being can also be interplanetary if it originates from a different planet

---

[43] extraterrestrial. (n.d.). *Dictionary.com Unabridged.* Retrieved May 29, 2014, from Dictionary.com website: http://dictionary.reference.com/browse/extraterrestrial

[44] interplanetary. (n.d.). *Dictionary.com Unabridged.* Retrieved May 29, 2014, from Dictionary.com website: http://dictionary.reference.com/browse/interplanetary

than Earth (extraterrestrial) and also has the capability to inhabit other planets (interplanetary).

Understanding this, we can throw in a couple more terms that will make the reading of this chapter easier. First is the term *"extradimensional"*, which would refer to something that originates from a different spatial dimension than the three we currently occupy. Next is *"interdimensional"*, which refers to something that has the capability to travel to other dimensions outside its own. For ease of reference and from here on out, I will refer to extraterrestrial beings as ETs and extradimensional beings as EDs.

The majority consensus concerning UFOs and the beings that pilot them is, if they exist at all, they are most likely ETs with interplanetary capabilities. What we want to be able to do is show that UFOs and their pilots are actually EDs. If we can show that, we can build a stronger case toward the idea that these beings are more likely fallen angels rather than ETs. There are a couple different ways to go about this.

The easiest way is by explaining the barrier of the speed of light. For example, the majority will find it easier to assume that supposed ETs would most likely originate from a different star system rather than our own solar system. If this assumption were true, the ETs would still have to abide by the cosmic speed limit put forth by Einstein. They should not be able to travel faster than light. This being the case, if ETs are from many light years away, they would have to travel immense speeds for impossible lengths of time to get here. The energy for this would be astronomical and, even then, the trip could take hundreds, thousands, or even millions of years. After explaining this, a little common sense can be implemented: it would seem if they were willing to spend that much time and energy in getting here, they would want to do more than secretly abduct people, flash bright lights at night, and steal our cows. This is a bit of a tongue-in-cheek response, but if done with care and not sarcasm, it can actually go a long way.

Almost always the very next thing that will come up is the idea of wormholes. The person defending the position of ETs is sure to state that if ETs are as technologically advanced as most people believe, they should have been able to find a way to bend space so the trip will not be as long. This is a commonly-held belief within the UFO community to explain how ETs can seem to arrive to our planet whenever they want.

Of course, there are problems with this idea as well. First, for ETs to bend space in that manner, they would need to traverse an extra dimension. This would mean they have interdimensional capabilities. They can still be considered as ETs if they originate from our three-dimensional universe, but we have to consider which is more likely. Is it easier to believe that ETs are so technologically advanced that they can pierce through a higher dimension, yet still want to bother with us? Or, is it easier to believe that these beings are actually *from* a higher dimension and travelling here would not be as much of a problem? Again, consider Flatland. If Flatlanders were actually real, we could be staring directly at one, mere millimeters from him and, as long as we are outside of his two-dimensional field of vision, he would never know it. Also, travel to the second dimension would require no technology whatsoever, as we could just stick our hand in to invade their space or physically pull the Flatlander out into ours.

Does this mean creating a wormhole or using a natural black hole to travel vast distances is impossible? It really all depends. With our current level of technology, it is impossible. Even with theoretically advanced technology, it is incredibly improbable. To quote Michio Kaku:

> *"However, with the wormhole and multiply connected spaces, we are probing the very limits of Einstein's theory of general relativity. In fact, the amount of matter-energy necessary to create a wormhole or dimensional gateway is so large that we expect quantum effects to dominate. Quantum corrections, in turn, may actually close the opening of the wormhole, making travel through the gateway impossible"*[45]

Many times, a person defending the ET position will want to use percentages and probabilities in their approach. I'm sure we are all familiar with the *"there are so many stars in the universe, it's next to impossible that not one has a planet with life"* argument. When this comes up, we must remember that we aren't debating the existence of life in the universe; we are trying to show the UFO phenomena is caused by EDs rather than ETs. Keeping that in mind as well as the high improbability of wormholes, we can use the same tactic to show our point. We just have to ask what is more likely? Does it seem probable that physical beings have been able to harness such immense energy, found a way to get around Einstein's theory completely, or can somehow

---

[45] Michio Kaku, *Hyperspace*, p. 231

survive the crushing force found within black hole-like conditions? Or, is it a more probable and simpler explanation that these beings are EDs, meaning none of these limitations would apply to them because they originate from a place of different physics than our own? A person cannot have it both ways; either they have to admit the probability of what you propose is much higher or they have to admit probabilities shouldn't factor in at all, thereby destroying their own argument. Either way, you are one step closer to opening this individual up to the truth.

The last thing I will bring up here is the technology aspect because it comes up quite often. It seems most individuals supporting the ET position will accept the notion that ETs possess near god-like technological capabilities that can get them out of any physical limitation. There is evidence to the contrary, however, showing these entities might not be as technologically advanced as they claim.

In a paper published in the Journal of Scientific Exploration, UFO researcher Jacques Vallee gave a few reasons why he believes UFOs are not extraterrestrial in origin.[46] In writing this, Jacques Vallee was coming from a secular worldview. He was not proposing anything from a Christian perspective. Vallee drew his conclusions based on the evidence he collected from various witnesses and other sources. He did not have what some would call a "Christian agenda".

The entire paper is fascinating and pretty spectacular given the end result goes against the grain of the mainstream view. Vallee makes

---

[46] Jacques F. Vallee, *Five Arguments Against the Extraterrestrial Origin of Unidentified Flying Objects,* Journal of Scientific Exploration, Vol. 4, No. 1, pp. 105-117, 1990, Pergamon Press plc. Printed in the USA

mention of five very good reasons against the idea that UFOs are extraterrestrial in nature. I will only mention a couple here, however I would suggest checking out the entire paper on your own.

One of the strongest points Vallee makes is that of the alien's physiology. They generally appear humanoid, meaning they have a head, body, two arms, two legs, and are bilaterally symmetrical. Vallee suggests that the fact something like this would happen under the current understanding of Darwinian evolution should stretch our understanding of biology past the limits. In other words, given all of the factors that Vallee lays out, it would be next to impossible for something so similar to evolve on a different planet than our own. If we consider this logically, Vallee has a point. How many humanoid creatures exist on our own planet compared against all creatures that don't possess a humanoid appearance? Again, it comes down to probability and Vallee poses the chances are astronomical at best.

Another point Vallee brings up is that of abduction reports. He shows how a majority of abductees claim to have intrusive medical procedures done on them by aliens while aboard a UFO. These medical procedures are usually incredibly painful, even to the point of leaving physical abrasions the next day. Many times, the abductees memory will be wiped clean, but it has been shown that, through hypnosis, some of these memories can be retrieved.

Vallee puts forth the observation that today, on our planet and in our culture, we have the medical advances available to us to be able to perform the same medical procedures without causing any pain to the person involved. Things like anesthesia can be used to ensure the person does not suffer and will not remember what happened. These procedures can be done without leaving the abrasions and scoop marks abductees have reported. They can even be done with a minimal amount of tools, meaning the person having the procedure done would not have to leave their house.

Given this, Vallee questions why technologically advanced ETs would need to take the individual aboard the UFO, subject them to all sorts of torturous experiences, and leave them with the evidence to show something had actually happened. If ETs are technologically advanced enough to get here from another planet, why are they lagging so far behind in their medical field? Perhaps it makes more sense that these beings are actually EDs who require no such extensive technology to travel here, are malevolent enough to not care about the well-being of those they abduct, and want to leave just enough evidence behind, enough times with enough people, to plant the idea in the minds of the general public that these things are happening.

Considering these beings as EDs will show their level of technology is above our own, however it seems to be lacking in certain areas that do not benefit them directly. If these beings are strictly malevolent in nature, they would not care to progress their technology to make the abductee comfortable or at ease. They would only progress their technology to suit their own needs, and that seems to be the case with the UFO phenomena.

One other point I will bring up is the nature of the reported UFOs. Many times, UFOs have been reported and even filmed to exhibit some seemingly impossible feats. UFOs sometimes split apart and come back together again, change shape and color as they hover in the sky, and even appear in two places at once. Remember back to our example of Flatland. What would it look like if a three-dimensional being traversed two-dimensional space? To a Flatlander, it would appear as a line or shape that is changing color, shape, and size. The three-dimensional object would appear and disappear, be in more than one place at one time, and seem to break every law of two-dimensional physics. Would it be reasonable for Flatlanders to assume that something exhibiting those behaviors is a super-advanced two-dimensional being, or would it make more sense that it is something from the third spatial dimension breaching their two-dimensional space?

Taking all of this into account, we can see how there are ways we can use scientific terminology, observations, and logic to make a strong case for EDs over ETs. Perhaps it's not that these things were just misunderstood technology in antiquity, as the ancient astronaut theory postulates. Perhaps it is that we are misunderstanding extradimensional manifestations today.

After showing all of this, it's just a matter of explaining how these manifestations were talked about in the ancient texts of the Bible. You can also use what we learned in the first chapter to explain why it seems ETs always preach New Age theology. Quite simply, it is because they are the same beings who originally perpetrated it ages ago. An individual who is heavily invested in the ETH (extraterrestrial hypothesis) most likely will not be convinced after one conversation, but it might be enough to plant a seed.

ETs in Hollywood

One of the latest and strangest phenomena that has been exponentially hitting our culture, and really the world, is the immense coverage and fictionalization of ETs in movies and television shows. It is a widely popular topic that earns a lot of money worldwide. There are countless television shows today popularizing the idea of ETs coming to Earth and comingling with humanity. Everything from Ancient Aliens on the History channel to Star-Crossed on the CW network covers this idea.

For us who recognize this topic for what it is, Genesis 6 immediately comes to mind. It seems like we are being prepared for something. It seems like the powers that be are preparing our minds for an eventuality. It is my personal belief that the popularity of this subject along with certain biblical and eschatological interpretations are no coincidence or chance-happening.

In deciding who to interview about this growing trend, I had a lot to consider. With topics like this, I think it best to start as close to the origin as possible. Of course, this all started way back in the time of Genesis 6 and I certainly cannot interview someone from that time. So, I had to think about my own journey. I had to ask myself, when was the first time I saw this type of thing popularized in the media?

My mind instantly jumped to a television show that was very popular when I was a child. The show was entitled *Alien Nation* and dealt with topics concerning the sociological issues surrounding the integration of an extraterrestrial race with humanity. As a child, I remember really loving the show.

Later on, I discovered a show entitled *V*. I soon found out that both shows, as well as many more, were created around the same time and by the same individual. This led me to the question, how did all of this biblical eschatology get mixed in shows like this, especially given how early on they were created?

Interview with Kenneth Johnson

Figure 19 - Kenneth Johnson is a producer, director, and writer for movies and television. He is the creator of V, Bionic Woman, Alien Nation, The Incredible Hulk, and other Emmy Award winning shows. He is the winner of the prestigious Viewers for Quality Television Award, multiple Saturn Awards, The Sci-Fi Universe Life Achievement Award, plus nominations for Writers Guild and Mystery Writers of America Award, among others.

In researching for this book, I decided to contact the creator of these shows, a man by the name of Kenneth Johnson (Figure 19), and ask questions that would hopefully lead to an answer for the integration of biblical and eschatological themes. To my delight, Mr. Johnson agreed to an interview for this book. Also, as an added bonus, Mr. Johnson proved to be incredibly forthcoming and helpful with his answers. While I do not personally agree with all of his views concerning religion, I would still like to state my heartfelt appreciation to Mr. Johnson for his honesty and willingness to take part in an interview such as this.

The interview with Kenneth Johnson was handled via email. What you see included in this book is the full content of my questions and Kenneth Johnson's answers. Only minor grammatical errors were corrected. Nothing else was changed. As far as what is revealed in terms of my original curiosity concerning biblical themes and eschatology in television shows, I believe the interview will speak for itself.

JOSH PECK: You have an impressive body of work, the majority of which is centered on directing and creating science fiction projects. What was your first introduction to the science fiction genre and what inspired you to make a career of it?

KENNETH JOHNSON: I never intended to have a "career" in science fiction. I have done many projects that were not in the area of sci-fi or even speculative fiction, but with my first major success creating *The Bionic Woman*, Hollywood was eager (as always) to find the best pigeon hole. I read a much greater spectrum of literary work throughout my youth, and was trained in the classic theater at Carnegie-Mellon's famed Department of Drama. I have tried to imbue all of my work in the sci-fi area with the traditions I learned from that classic literature.

JOSH PECK: You are usually most recognized in the sci-fi community for your creation of *V: The Original Miniseries*, and interestingly enough, *V* was not originally meant to be a sci-fi production. Can you speak about your original vision for *V*, how it became science fiction, and how much of the sci-fi elements after the conversion you were personally responsible for?

KENNETH JOHNSON: As is fairly well known, I was inspired by Sinclair Lewis's 1930's novel, *It Can't Happen Here* to create a work where suddenly in contemporary America we were living under a totalitarian regime. I wanted to explore how ordinary people would react to extraordinary circumstances.

The original project was entirely Earth-based, about a grassroots fascist takeover of our country by impassioned people living here. NBC loved the idea but wanted an outside force to be responsible for the takeover. I did not believe any nation could accomplish such a power grab and we ultimately decided that it should be a supremely powerful force from another world. I thus was responsible for creating that alien force and determining all the characteristics of their race and society.

JOSH PECK: It seems many of the projects you have been involved in have to do with themes concerning extraterrestrial life.

What are your personal beliefs/views/opinions about the existence of life elsewhere in the universe and have any of your personal beliefs been reflected in your work?

KENNETH JOHNSON: To set the record straight, of all my many projects only two have dealt with ETs... *V* and *Alien Nation*. My feeling is simply that the universe is so incomprehensibly vast that to presume we are the only sentient creatures is the height of human egoism.

JOSH PECK: Have you or anyone you know ever experienced or witnessed anything that would be considered extraterrestrial or paranormal before, and if so, has it motivated your work in any way?

KENNETH JOHNSON: Nope.

JOSH PECK: There is a widely accepted and growing belief in the ufology community about a species of extraterrestrial known as *"Reptilians"*, usually referred to as the most feared, powerful, and even evil species of all known extraterrestrials. This belief sometimes even states the Reptilians are living on Earth disguised as human beings. Were you or anyone involved in the creation of *V* aware of the belief in the Reptilians, did it play a part in deciding the *V* aliens' appearance, and if not, what was the original inspiration to make the *V* aliens reptilian under human skin in appearance as opposed to other looks more popular at the time, such as the "gray" or "little green men from Mars" look?

KENNETH JOHNSON: George Burns once told me, "When you're going to tell a lie put as much truth in is as you can." In *V* it is literally stated by the anthropologist Robert Maxwell that *"...A reptilian race could easily have evolved right here on Earth..."* because until 65 million years ago the reptiles ruled. Then the great meteor impact altered Earth's climate and the biggest and smartest died off.

JOSH PECK: What part, if any, did you have in the television remake of *V*?

KENNETH JOHNSON: None. I received a "Created by" credit because per the WGA agreement all writers and studios are subject to, Warners was obligated to list that credit. I had no input in the 1985 series nor the short-lived 2009 version.

JOSH PECK: Was the remake of *V* portrayed to your liking and what would you have liked seen done differently?

KENNETH JOHNSON: I only saw the pilot. It was not at all my cup of tea. I was very pleased that they had not used any of my original characters or storylines. -- The viewing audience, unfortunately, was not pleased and the excellent first-night ratings dropped like a rock the second week and continued to fall off in what *Fortune* magazine characterized as a *"precipitous decline."*

JOSH PECK: You were one of the first to acknowledge the potential social issues connected with the cohabitation of humans and aliens with *Alien Nation*. What was your motivation for addressing these issues?

KENNETH JOHNSON: I was raised in a very bigoted, ante-Semitic household and for some reason I never bought into it. Throughout my career I have tried to seize every opportunity to chip away at such intolerance and prejudice. Fox had an unsuccessful feature titled *Alien Nation* and asked me to look at it because they thought it might still be a decent TV series -- sort of *Lethal Weapon* with aliens. -- What I saw was the possibility of doing *In the Heat of The Night* -- a series about racial discrimination.

JOSH PECK: Serious talks of the social, political, and spiritual issues connected with alien/human cohabitation and breeding are increasing in popularity today and are constantly being addressed in television shows such as *Ancient Aliens*. What are your thoughts on this growing trend and, being you were one of the first in the entertainment industry to bring these ideas to light, have your personal views on alien/human cohabitation and breeding influenced any of your work? If so, in what way?

KENNETH JOHNSON: See above. -- And also note that in my novel *V The Second Generation* I created an entire sub-species of Visitor-human half-breeds so that I could continue to explore (and condemn) intolerance.

JOSH PECK: In the field of eschatology, especially in the Bible-based Christian community, there is a growing belief that deceptive fallen angels masquerading as extraterrestrials will be a fulfillment of Bible prophecy in the very near future. Within this community, some have noted that shows such as *Alien Nation* and especially *V* contain many specific themes, elements, and even minute details that directly line up and agree with their pre-established interpretations of Bible prophecy. Were you aware of these prophetic interpretations, are the numerous and specific similarities just coincidence, and have you used the Bible or any other kind of spiritual outlet as inspiration for any of your work?

KENNETH JOHNSON: Certainly Biblical references -- and all other similarly mythological writings -- have had various influences upon me and most writers. But there has never been any conscious research or desire on my part to "align" with or reflect any religious dogma.

My personal feeling is much in line with John Lennon and the legions of others who believe that virtually all religion has provided most of the darkest chapters of misery and murder in all of human history. I would urge all people to read *The Age of Reason* written by the great American patriot Thomas Paine in the 1790's. An honest assessment of that short work will cause a thinking person to totally reevaluate giving credence, faith and -- oh yes -- money to any religious creed or sect.

JOSH PECK: There were talks about the possibility of you creating a new *V* movie. Is this project still a possibility, and if so, where can people find more information about you, your work, and your future projects?

KENNETH JOHNSON: Yes. We are working hard to get a remake of my original *V* before the cameras as a major motion picture. It would be the first of a trilogy. See the information at www.kennethjohnson.us.

* * *

A very special thanks goes out to Kenneth Johnson for sharing his unique perspective and experience in this interview.

Chapter 6

Basics of Ten-Dimensional Theory

For by him were all things created, that are in heaven, and that are in

earth, visible and invisible, whether they be thrones, or dominions, or

principalities, or powers: all things were created by him, and for him:

Colossians 1:16 (KJV)

Above the Fourth

Until now, we have primarily been focusing on the fourth spatial dimension and a few of its possible biblical implications. Next in our journey through the exciting world of modern physics, we will look at the theoretical dimensions above the fourth spatial.[47] For this chapter, we will be primarily defining the ten

---

[47] While I maintain at least the fourth spatial dimension as synonymous with the spiritual world and thus biblical fact, I'm not entirely sure about saying the same for the rest. There are minor clues throughout the Bible that could be indirectly pointing to higher dimensions above the fourth spatial, but saying so would be highly speculative at best. It is my position that, while these topics are certainly interesting and they could prove to be true in the future, the best we can do for now is allow our imaginations to wander and ponder the great "what if" questions while keeping in mind there is no absolute proof, scientific nor biblical, to substantiate nor debunk these theoretical answers.

spatial dimensions proposed by modern physicists. We will touch a bit on the idea of time as the first temporal dimension here, however we will delve deeper into the riddles of time in another chapter.

Planck Boundaries

Before we can probe deeper into the fifth spatial dimension and beyond, we must understand the meaning of the term *"Planck boundary"*. Planck boundaries come up time and again in various attempts to describe some of the strange properties higher dimensions might have. Planck boundaries are so important, in fact, that they have the potential to define the exact amount of separation between our physical world and the spiritual world.

Max Karl Ernst Ludwig Planck (April 23, 1858 – October 4, 1947) made incredible contributions to physics throughout his life (Figure 20). Planck, a German theoretical physicist, founded quantum theory in 1900 and actually coined the term *"quantum"*. He is also known for developing the *"Plank constant"*, which is a physical constant that describes the quanta of action in quantum mechanics.[48] In 1918, Planck received the Nobel Prize in physics for his discovery of energy quanta. It is with the Planck Constant that Planck boundaries can be determined.

---

[48] The term *"quanta"* (plural of *"quantum"*) defines the smallest amount of measurement possible for any given thing, such as length, energy, time, etc.

The Planck constant is so important in reconciling modern physics with the Bible because it shows there is a type of natural

measurement scale in which everything within physical existence adheres. We can actually determine the units of measurement God used to create the universe. Having this scale is comparable to possessing God's personal tape measure, thermometer, and stopwatch.

Figure 20 - Max Planck in 1933

The Planck length is also important to modern quantum physics because it is the only length that could naturally appear in a quantum theory of gravity, and gravity is connected to the shape of space. However, for our purposes here, you only need to know that the Planck length (the unit of measurement in God's scale) is incredible small; subatomic in fact. It is so incredibly small that it is nearly impossible to fathom. The Planck length is one thousandth of a millionth of a trillionth of a centimeter. It is usually represented as 10^{-33} cm in size, which is about twenty-four orders of magnitude smaller than an atom and nineteen orders of magnitude smaller than a proton.[49] In order to put this into perspective, consider this example from Wikipedia:

---

[49] 10^{-33} (stated as "ten to the negative thirty-third power") is an expression of scientific notation, which is an easier way to express extremely cumbersome numbers. When a power of ten has a negative exponent, it indicates a decimal number, therefore 10^{-33} is the number 0.000,000,000,000,000,000,000,000,000,000,001. A number with a positive

The size of the Planck length can be visualized as follows: if a particle or dot about 0.1mm in size (which is at or near the smallest the unaided human eye can see) were magnified in size to be as large as the observable universe, then inside that universe-sized "dot", the Planck length would be roughly the size of an actual 0.1mm dot. In other words, the diameter of the observable universe is to within less than an order of magnitude, larger than a 0.1 millimeter object, roughly at or near the limits of the unaided human eye, by about the same factor (10^{31}) as that 0.1mm object or dot is larger than the Planck length. More simply – on a logarithmic scale, a dot is halfway between the Planck length and the size of the observable universe.[50]

In other words, if you were shrunk down to a Planck length, the diameter of the period at the end of this sentence would still be about 3 ½ times longer than the diameter of the observable universe in relation. Not only did God create things so large that we don't know exactly where they end (i.e. the universe), He used a scale with units of measurements so small that we have trouble even fathoming it.

---

exponent indicates how many zeroes come after the 1. For example, 10^{33} is just a shorter way of writing the number 1,000,000,000,000,000,000,000,000,000,000,000. An order of magnitude is a factor of ten. Twenty-four orders of magnitude is 1,000,000,000,000,000,000,000,000, or one trillion trillion, or 10^{24} (a number 1 with twenty-four zeroes after it).

[50] http://en.wikipedia.org/wiki/Planck_length

CHAPTER 6

What is really interesting about the Planck length is what happens when something even smaller is attempted to be considered. Physicist Lisa Randall explains:

"The Planck scale energy – the energy needed to explore the Planck scale length – is exactly the energy at which gravity is no longer dismissible as a feeble force. At the Planck scale length, gravity cannot be ignored. In fact, at the Plank scale energy, gravity constructs barriers that make conventional quantum mechanical calculations impossible. Anything sufficiently energetic to probe 10^{-33}cm would be snapped up into a black hole that imprisons whatever enters."[51]

Nothing smaller than a Planck length is possible because it would require energy larger than is calculably fathomable. This brings us to Planck energy.

While most measurements corresponding to the Planck constant are incredibly small (such as Planck length, mass, and time), the measurement of energy at the Planck scale is incredibly large. The Planck scale of energy is around 1.22×10^{19} GeV. In this equation, GeV represents gigaelectronvolts, or one billion electronvolts. An electronvolt (usually represented as eV) is a unit of energy equal to approximately 1.6×10^{-19} joule (joule is usually represented as J). By comparison, one 100 watt light bulb turned on for one minute equals

---

[51] Lisa Randall, *Warped Passages: Unraveling the Mysteries of the Universe's Hidden Dimensions*, © 2005, HarperCollins Publishers, 280.

about 6,000 joules.[52] Therefore, the Planck energy scale is incredibly large. With numbers such as this, it begins to make sense why such an extreme amount of energy needed to probe the Planck length would result in a black hole.

A similar result is theorized when dealing with mass on the Planck scale. Planck mass is the maximum allowed mass for quanta. In other words, it's the most amount possible for the smallest thing possible. This type of mass isn't as impossible to imagine, although the actual size of quanta can be. Unlike all other Planck base units and most Planck derived units, the Planck mass has a scale more or less conceivable to humans. Planck mass is usually expressed as 2.17645×10^{-8} kg (whereas kg represents kilograms). It is traditionally said to be about the mass of a flea, but more accurately it is about the mass of a flea egg.[53] It is said, much like when dealing with the Planck length, that if two quanta of the Planck mass or greater ever met, they could spontaneously form a black hole. It is interesting how the consequence of a black hole comes up in regards to Planck boundaries. It is almost as if black holes are a natural type of fail-safe system that God put in place to keep our reality within the appropriate boundaries necessary for physical reality to be possible.

---

[52] We measure watts as equal to joules per second. 1 watt is equal to 1 joule per 1 second. Therefore, 100 watts equals 100 joules per second. Multiply 100 joules per second by 60 (for 60 seconds in one minute), and you arrive at 6,000 joules for 100 watts at one minute.

[53] http://en.wikipedia.org/wiki/Planck_mass

CHAPTER 6

That brings us to the last Planck measurement we will look at in this chapter: that of time. Planck time is measured as the time required for light to travel a distance of one Planck length within a vacuum. This is the absolute shortest amount of time that is possible. It equates out to be 5.39121×10^{-44} s (whereas s represents seconds). It is usually approximated as 10^{-43} seconds for ease of reference. This is an incredibly short period of time; it is one that is inconceivable to our human mind and one that is far from observable. To put this in perspective, as of May 2010, the smallest time interval ever directly measured is 12 attoseconds (1.2×10^{-17} seconds), which equals to 3.7×10^{26} Planck times.[54]

There are deeper implications of Planck time that could be discussed, but for our purposes here, it is only important to know that this shows time as being quite different than what we may have imagined. We normally would think of time like a constantly flowing river. In reality, however, time is more like a film strip or stack of photographs. Each snapshot encompasses the entire physical universe and represents one Planck time. Our journey through time is nothing more than quickly flipping through these snapshots. Every passing second is made up of billions of billions of billions of Planck time snapshots. In fact, there are more units of Planck time in one second than there are seconds contained in the 14 billion years since the

---

[54] http://www.physorg.com/news192909576.html - *"12 attoseconds is the world record for shortest controllable time"*, 2010-05-12. Retrieved 2012-04-19 at http://en.wikipedia.org/wiki/Planck_time

scientifically-proposed beginning the universe.[55] When we really think about how constraining time really is, it can help us put into perspective the biblical notions of God existing outside of time (though He does choose to enter the boundaries of time here and there), His ability to see the beginning from the end, and the ultimate beauty of His creative nature.[56]

Higher Dimensions: Rolled Up or Infinite?

Now that we have a basic understanding of some of the more fundamental qualities of Planck boundaries, we can begin to look at higher dimensions from the scope of modern theoretical physics. There are two primary beliefs about the capacity and location of higher dimensions. The first states that spatial dimensions above the third are "rolled up" and the second states they might be infinite in size.

The idea that a higher spatial dimension could be rolled up is not exactly new. Theodor Kaluza was a German physicist and mathematician who came up with what is known as the Kaluza-Klein theory (or KK theory). This theory uses five dimensions (four of space and one of time) to mathematically unify the force of gravity with the

---

[55] Though I am only using this as an example, I feel it is important to point out that I do tend to favor the side of Young Earth Creation, which states God created everything roughly six thousand years ago within six literal 24-hour days. I am not dogmatic about this belief. I believe Old Earth Creation is a valid viewpoint for Christians to have should they so choose. Personally, I see more biblical and scientific evidence pointing toward a young Earth, however I do not believe this should ever become a point of contention or cause division within the Church.

[56] Isaiah 46:9-11

force of electromagnetism. This theory was first published in 1921 and would later pave the way for modern day string theory.

In 1926, Oskar Klein proposed that the fourth spatial dimension is curled up in such a way that if a particle were to travel along it, the particle would end up right where it began. Physicist Peter Freund explains it as such:

"Think of some imaginary people living in Lineland, which consists of a single line. Throughout their history, they believed that their world was just a single line. Then, a scientist in Lineland proposed that their world was not just a one-dimensional line, but a two-dimensional world. When asked where this mysterious and unobservable second dimension was, he would reply that the second dimension was curled up into a small ball. Thus, the line people actually live on the surface of a long, but very thin, cylinder. The radius of the cylinder is too small to be measured; it is so small, in fact, that it appears that the world is just a line."[57]

Physicist Michio Kaku then picks up the explanation where Freund leaves off:

"If the radius of the cylinder were larger, the line people could move off their universe and move perpendicular to their line world. In other words, they could perform interdimensional travel. As they moved perpendicular to Lineland, they would encounter an infinite number of parallel line worlds that coexisted with their universe. As

---

[57] Michio Kaku, *Hyperspace*, 105-106

they moved farther into the second dimension, they would eventually return to their own line world. Now think of Flatlanders living on a plane. Likewise, a scientist on Flatland may make the outrageous claim that traveling through the third dimension is possible. In principle, a Flatlander could rise off the surface of Flatland. As this Flatlander slowly floated upward into the third dimension, his "eyes" would see an incredible sequence of different parallel universes, each coexisting with this universe. Because his eyes would be able to see parallel to the surface of Flatland, he would see different Flatland universes appearing before him."[58]

We can take those lower-dimensional principles and apply them to our own reality. In Lineland, if their only perception of a second spatial dimension came in the form of it being curled up into a two-dimensional cylinder the size of the Planck length, the extra dimension would still be there, it would just be too small for the Linelanders to be able to perceive it.[59] This is the same idea that Klein proposed about the fourth spatial dimension. If the next spatial dimension up were curled in a ball the size of a Planck length, it would be too small for us to detect. This is the same logic that is sometimes used to describe the rest of the ten spatial dimensions in physics today.

---

[58] Ibid. 106

[59] The interesting thing about this is for a 2 dimensional plane to be curled up, it would require the space of a third spatial dimension to do it in. Following this logic, if the fourth spatial dimension was curled up into a ball, it would require the space of a fifth spatial dimension to do it in, so on and so forth.

CHAPTER 6

Many Worlds Interpretation

This is what brings us to the idea of parallel dimensions, or what is sometimes known as *"many worlds"* or *"relative state formulation"*. It was American physicist Hugh Everett III who came up with the original relative state formulation in 1957. It was later named the *"many worlds interpretation"* (or simply MWI) in the 1960s and 1970s by Bryce Seligman DeWitt. This theory basically states that in universes parallel to our own, anything that could have happened in fact did. In other words, for every choice any given person could have made and for every accidental occurrence of anything at all, there would somewhere be a parallel universe to manifest it. This theory states there are multiple versions of you, me, and everyone else inhabiting parallel universes, some nearly identical to our own and some wildly different. The number of parallel universes is theorized to be infinite. Much like the idea that a Linelander would experience an infinite number of one-dimensional lines comprising the second spatial dimension, or a Flatlander would experience an infinite number of two-dimensional planes comprising the third spatial dimension, the theory states there could be an infinite number of three-dimensional universes comprising the fourth spatial dimension.

On the surface, there are some theological problems with this theory that make most Christians dismiss it as a ridiculous fantasy. Questions come up, for example, like "if there are infinite versions of myself out there, wouldn't that mean there are some universes where I have never and will never accept Jesus as my Savior?" and "If every time I make a choice, a parallel version of myself is making the opposite choice, doesn't that negate free will?" as well as many others.

I believe these are very valid questions that deserve an answer, but I do not believe these questions alone are grounds to dismiss the many worlds theory completely. I will state up front that I do not believe there are multiple versions of ourselves out there and I will explain why briefly a bit later. First, let's imagine hypothetically that one day in the future it is proven there are, in fact, parallel universes and they do contain multiple versions of ourselves. Should this be enough to shake our faith? Does this type of conclusion negate God completely? Of course not. It would only prove that God's creation is far more complex than we originally thought. To briefly answer the two questions from the beginning of the previous paragraph: yes, it would probably mean there are other versions of ourselves that are not saved, but this would be on a purely biological level. We have to remember, these parallel universes would still be constrained to three dimensions of space. The other "you" might look and sound like you, but they would still have a separate spirit and soul that is unshared. This also answers the second question of free will. It does not negate your personal free will because you still have the choice to do whatever you want, even if the other "you" chooses something different. They would be doing so completely independent of you, and you completely independent of them. This type of theory is nothing that should make us question our faith in God or knowledge of His creation.

While I do not believe there are multiple versions of ourselves out there, I do believe it is at least possible there are multiple universes. My reasons for this are simple. Think back to the Flatlander lifting off into the third spatial dimension. As he moves through our reality, he is confronted with a seemingly infinite amount of parallel two-dimensional planes; he sees an infinite number of other Flatlands. These parallel Flatlands, in three-dimensional reality, are nothing more than the two-dimensional planes stacked up to create three-dimensional objects. They do not need to be inhabited in order for them to exist. If the Flatlander were rising up while viewing my coffee mug, he would see a seemingly infinite number of curved lines representing circular planes that make up the coffee mug. Some of these two-dimensional Flatland universes would be perfectly circular, while others would contain another section as he moved to view the handle of the mug. He might even notice the lines that represent the kitchen wall behind the coffee mug. That doesn't mean each of these planes must be inhabited by other Flatlanders. Quite the contrary, these stacked up planes are just what make up our three-dimensional reality.

I am more inclined to understand the fourth spatial dimension (and higher dimensions) in the same way. It makes perfect sense to me that theoretically the fourth spatial dimension could be made up of a seemingly infinite number of "stacked up" three-dimensional objects, but that in no way would indicate these other three-dimensional worlds are inhabited by other versions of ourselves. It would just be the make-up of the fourth spatial dimension. I believe some of these hypothetical parallel universes would look very similar to our own while others would look very different, but I do not believe any of them would have to be inhabited by other three-dimensional beings.

Here is another way to think of this; imagine what it would take for a Flatlander to have parallel versions of himself. The only way this would be possible is if the Flatlander himself was made of stacked up two-dimensional planes. In other words, the Flatlander would have to be three-dimensional. If the Flatlander is three-dimensional, that automatically negates the possibility of there being a separate two-dimensional version of himself, because he himself is already of the next dimension up. For example, if one were to try and remove a two-dimensional section from the middle of the now-three-dimensional former Flatlander, one would be slicing the former Flatlander in half, thereby killing him and ending his three-dimensional existence altogether. Therefore, if other three-dimensional universes were inhabited, it seems we would be four-dimensional in nature, and our "three-dimensional parallel selves" would actually be a part of our four-dimensional make-up.

As a quick side-note, this might be what people are experiencing when they report supposed ghost sightings or demon manifestations. It could be that the seemingly three-dimensional form is actually just one cross-section of their four-dimensional body that is seen briefly in our dimension. That might also help explain what Paul meant when he wrote *"Satan himself is transformed into an angel of light"*.[60] Of course, this is just speculation, but it is at least interesting to consider.

There is another version of many worlds that states all of the infinite versions of ourselves actually exist in our own universe. This is an older theory that has since all but fizzled out. It was based on the assumption that our physical universe is infinite in size. Because there are only a certain number of particles in existence and only a certain amount of ways they can be arranged, the mathematics would suggest

---

[60] 2 Corinthians 11:14

that if our universe were truly infinite in size, there would have to be other Earths out there with other versions of ourselves. This would actually be true if the universe was truly infinite.[61] The way to show that our three-dimensional universe is not infinite is by the fact that it is expanding. In fact, it is expanding at an exponential rate, faster and faster. Nobody knows exactly why this is occurring, but it does show that the universe cannot be truly infinite. If it were, there would be nowhere for the universe to expand. The universe would be stationary, or what is known as a *"static universe"*. However, that is not what is observed. The fact that our universe is expanding would seem to show that what we observe in our three spatial dimensions is not all there is. However, somewhere there is a boundary. Now, what that boundary looks like and what lays beyond is completely speculative and is something we will discuss in more detail later in this book, but the fact that the universe is not infinite in size is important to know in moving forward on our journey to understanding higher dimensions.

There is another explanation theorized by physicist Lisa Randall that might allow for the fourth spatial dimension to be infinite in size. This was previously thought impossible due to the idea that if higher dimensions were infinite in size, gravity should be completely different than what we observe. Randall poses an idea concerning *"localized gravity"* in her book *Warped Passages*. This is a theory that answers the

---

[61] We must remember, when dealing with a term like "infinite", we are dealing with something that has no end. Half of infinity is still infinity. Given that, and given the fact that the number of particles that make up matter and their arrangements is finite, all possible outcomes would have to be made manifest in a truly infinite universe.

gravity problem while maintaining the possibility that the fourth spatial dimension could be infinite in size rather than rolled up to Planck length size. This is especially interesting because, if ever proven to be true, it would give physics a new view of the fourth spatial dimension that may actually fall closer in line with biblical descriptions of spiritual existence. It is speculative at this point, but the mathematics seem to allow for the possibility. It is an interesting consideration at the very least.

Significance of Twelve

The basic higher-dimensional theory of today is that there exists ten spatial dimensions plus one temporal dimension. Sometimes the *"zeroth"* dimension is added to explain where the original starting point is in defining dimensions.[62] If this is the correct definition of everything within God's creation, it would bring the total number to twelve dimensions (one zeroth dimension, one of time, and ten of space), which has special and specific biblical implications.

The number twelve is very important in the Bible and always seems to convey the same idea of order, perfection, and divine government. For example, Jacob had twelve sons who became the twelve patriarchs of Israel (Genesis 49-28). Twelve stones were attached to the breastplate of the priest in correspondence to the twelve tribes (Exodus 39:8-14). Solomon had twelve officers over all of Israel (1

---

[62] If the first spatial dimension is defined as a single line between two points, it is sometimes said that a dimension of zero would have to exist to contain the original first point. Once a second point is added, it automatically becomes the first spatial dimension.

Kings 4:7). Omri reigned over Israel for twelve years (1 Kings 16:23), as did Jehoram (2 Kings 3:1). Manasseh was twelve years old when he began to reign (2 Kings 21:1). The altar in Ezekiel 43:18 is measured as twelve cubits long and twelve cubits broad, which would equate to 144 square cubits.[63]

In the New Testament, the woman with the issue of blood was afflicted for twelve years before being healed (Matthew 9:20). Jesus had twelve disciples (Matthew 10:1). Jesus said if He prayed for it, God would deliver Him more than twelve legions of angels (Matthew 26:53). Jesus was twelve years old when He taught for the first time (Luke 2:42). The woman clothed with the sun had a crown of twelve stars (Revelation 12:1). The number twelve shows up all over in descriptions of the New Jerusalem (Revelation 21:12-22:2). Of course, there are many other examples we could look at, but this is more than enough to show the significance of the number twelve in the Bible.

Given this, it would make biblical sense if there are twelve dimensions in total. Twelve shows perfect order. Being that we are talking about God's creation, and the fact that *it was good* before sin was introduced (Genesis 1:4), it would be reasonable to assume that God would have created everything expressing a perfect order. Of course, this strays from what we can consider as biblical fact and falls more in line with speculation. If true, it could help explain some things and show

---

[63] This also points to the 144,000 in the book of Revelation. It says that 12,000 come from each of the twelve tribes.

that God's creation is far more expansive and amazing than what we originally may have thought.

Imagining the Spatial and the Temporal

There is an alternative method of visualizing higher dimensions that may prove useful. This method comes from visualizing all the dimensions as stories of a building (Figure 21). In most instances, time

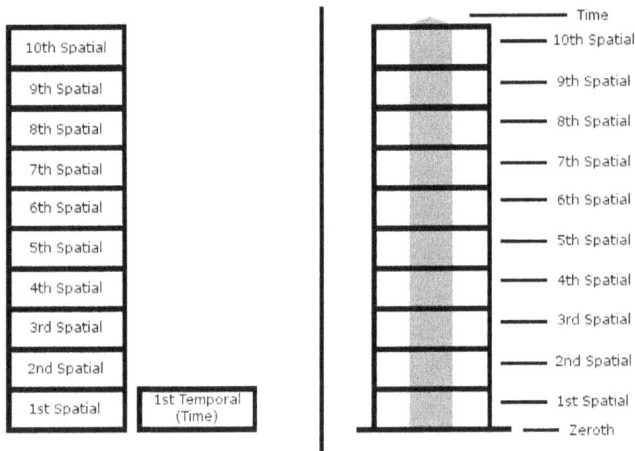

Figure 21 - The example to the left shows how time is sometimes seen as a separate type of dimension from the ten spatial dimensions. However, a more accurate portrayal might be the example to the right, that shows time integrated into the spatial dimensions with the zeroth as their foundation.

is seen as a completely separate type of building, only one-story high, next to a ten-story tall building.[64] However, if we are to think of time as an attribute of every spatial dimension, we could think of time as the

---

[64] Of course, this is done only in principle. As Einstein showed, time is generally accepted as being woven into space, known as *"space-time"*. In trying to define dimensions, however, time is sometimes seen as a separate type of dimension than that of space. Other times, they are referred to as *"spacetime dimensions"*, in which case there would be only ten, such as in *The Hidden Reality* by Brian Greene, pages 96-97.

elevator shaft that connects all of the spatial dimensions. If we consider the zeroth dimension as relevant, we could think of that as the foundation in which the building rests upon. This can give us a complete picture of the ten spatial dimensions, time, and the zeroth dimension. If we look at it that way, we have a way of imagining the twelve total theoretical dimensions that make up all of reality.

Of course, the question *"Where is God in all of this?"* might come up. God Himself was present before anything else. He created everything, including all conceivable dimensions. This would mean that God would have to be outside of this entire twelve-dimensional system. God does not originate from any dimension. He created all dimensions. He has the ability to enter any dimension at will. To ask *"What dimension is God in?"* misses the entire point. God is outside of all time and spatial dimension. Heaven, on the other hand, being a part of God's creation, might exist in one of the higher dimensions. This, of course, is speculative.

Learning these things and trying to imagine them is, at the very least, a fun exercise in bending the mind to consider things we don't observably encounter or interact with on a day to day basis. More important than that, however, is it is a great way to gain appreciation for the majesty and magnitude of God's creation in all its forms. Through this, we can begin to understand what Paul was talking about when he wrote:

"For the invisible things of him from the creation of the world are clearly seen, being understood by the things that are made, even his eternal power and Godhead; so that they are without excuse:"[65]

The more time goes by and the more we can discover about the complexities surrounding God's creation, the less excuse we have for not giving Him the credit He deserves. In short, it is unfair and unreasonable to take the Creator out of His creation. The more we realize concerning what He did, however, the more it provides us with limitless bounds of intrigue and awe.

---

[65] Romans 1:20 KJV

Chapter 7

The Building Blocks of Reality

I will praise thee; for I am fearfully and wonderfully made: marvellous
are thy works; and that my soul knoweth right well.

Psalm 139:14 (KJV)

The Strange World of Particle Physics

The studies of particle physics and quantum mechanics are fascinating ones indeed. They are the studies of the literal building blocks of matter and energy. They are a direct look into the materials God used in His creation. They define a world so strangely different than our own, yet is what makes up our own. It is a world full of unpredictable behaviors and head-spinning contradictions. If there is anything in the world that has the potential to instill an automatic humility in a person, it is the study of the building blocks of the world itself. Just when humanity thinks they have a fair grasp on reality, something else is discovered that throws everything else for a loop. Proverbs 25:2 states *"It is the glory of God to conceal a thing: but the honour of kings is to search out a matter"*, and that is especially true in this area of study.

Until now, we have primarily looked at things that are theoretical in nature. No one has been able to scientifically observe a higher dimension or anything of the kind. We will get back into theoretical issues, but for now it will serve our purposes well to define some of the things that have been scientifically observed and measured. It is the attributes and behaviors of these building blocks that lead to theories concerning things of an even smaller magnitude, even down to Planck length size.

Some of the things discussed in this chapter might bring you back to the days of high school science class. Some may not. However, do not be mistaken. This will not be your average lesson in the basics of particle physics. There are things I will present here that you may find utterly shocking. For the benefit of the reader, I will cover only the essentials to understanding the rest of this book and hopefully provoke further study on your own in any given area. Usually when these types of explanations are done, they begin with larger particles and work down to the smallest. However, since the larger particles are actually made of the smaller ones, I believe the best way to begin is to start with the smallest and work our way up from there.

Fermions and Bosons

These are the most fundamental and basic building blocks known. As stated above, some might point out that the molecule or atom would be a better place to start, but I find explaining what a molecule is while possessing knowledge of the atom and its constructs is far easier than explaining what a molecule is with no knowledge of the atom and its constructs. Thus, we begin here.

CHAPTER 7

Fermions and bosons are what is known as *"elementary particles"*. These are the smallest particles we know in existence. Anything smaller than these elementary particles is theoretical. Fermions are generally matter particles while bosons are generally force particles.[66] The job of bosons is to determine interactions among fermions.

Probably the most well-known fermion is the quark. Quarks are of the smallest particles known, however one would not find a quark on its own. Quarks combine to create what are called hadrons. Hadrons themselves can be either composite fermions or composite bosons. If a hadron is a composite fermion, it is known as a baryon. If a hadron is a composite boson, it is known as a meson.

There are six different types of quarks. These types are called flavors. They are up, down, strange, charm, bottom, and top. Up and down quarks are known as first generation quarks, strange and charm are second generation, and bottom and top are third. For every quark flavor, there is also a corresponding antiquark. Up and down quarks have the lowest mass and are the most stable of all the quarks. Strange, charm, bottom, and top quarks are less stable and can only be produced through high energy collisions, such as cosmic rays and particle accelerators.[67]

---

[66] Matter particles would include quarks and leptons while force particles would include gauge bosons and the Higgs bosons. Interestingly enough, even antimatter particles, such as antiquarks and antileptons, would be considered as fermions.

[67] The Large Hadron Collider at CERN is an example of this.

Quarks also have different types of electrical charge. Depending on the quark, the charge is either $+\frac{2}{3}$ or $-\frac{1}{3}$ of the elementary charge.[68] Up, charm, and top quarks (which are referred to as up-type quarks) have a charge of $+\frac{2}{3}$, while down, strange, and bottom quarks (known as down-type quarks) have $-\frac{1}{3}$ (Figure 22). Antiquarks, on the other hand, have the opposite charge to their corresponding quarks. Up-type antiquarks have charges of $-\frac{2}{3}$ while down-type antiquarks have charges of $+\frac{1}{3}$.

Charge	First Gen.	Second Gen.	Third Gen.
$+2/3$	u up quark	c charm quark	t top quark
$-1/3$	d down quark	s strange quark	b bottom quark
	less mass		more mass

Figure 22 - Chart showing the generations, charge, and relative mass of all six quark flavors.

There is much, much more we could get into concerning the complexities of quarks. They have far more attributes and strangeness than what we can cover within this one book. For our purposes here, however, we have covered enough to understand the rest.

Nucleons

In simple language, nucleons are what the nucleus of atoms are made of. There are two known types of nucleons: neutrons and protons. These nucleons bind together to form the atomic nucleus. Most examples and models of nucleons show them as different colored balls stuck together (Figure 24). However, this type of model isn't exactly accurate. In reality, strangely enough, each nucleon would be in multiple

---

[68] An elementary charge is the electric charge carried by a single proton, or the opposite of the electric charge carried by an electron.

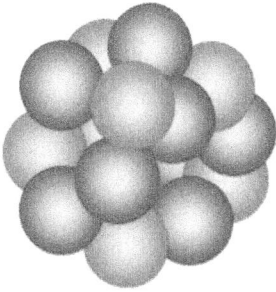

Figure 24 - *An example of an atomic nucleus with the differently colored balls representing protons and neutrons.*

places at once spread throughout the nucleus. Of course, there is really no good way to model something that bizarre.

Protons are made up of three quarks: two up quarks and one down quark, whereas neutrons are made of two down quarks and one up quark (Figure 23). Protons have a positive electric charge of one elementary charge. Neutrons, on the other hand, have no electric charge (hence the name "neutron" as they are neutral). The mass of a neutron is slightly more than a proton. The nucleus of every atom consists of at least one neutron and one or more protons.[69]

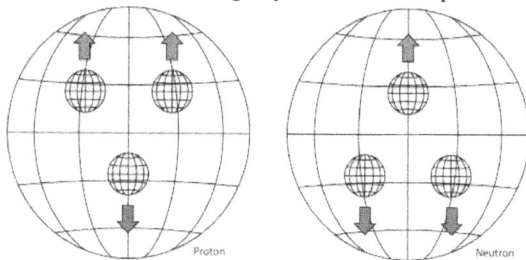

Figure 23 - *The proton and neutron with corresponding quarks.*

Electrons

Now that we know what the nucleus of an atom consists of, we can look at the other part of an atom: the electron. Electrons are strange subatomic particles indeed. They have a negative elementary charge and their mass is only about 1/1836 that of a proton. To put that in perspective, it is the same weight relation as a two-month old kitten to an average-sized car.

---

[69] The one exception to this is hydrogen-1 (sometimes known as protium) which consists of only a single proton.

The electron was once recognized as an elementary particle because it had no known substructure. In essence, it was thought to be made of nothing at all. As early as 1980, it was thought that the electron could be made of three different components. These three components were theorized as being a spinon (providing spin), an orbiton (providing the orbit) and a holon (carrying the electric charge). In 1996, physicist seemed to split the electron into a holon and spinon; then in 2012 Swiss and German researchers observed a split of the electron into a spinon and orbiton.[70]

In 1913, fascinated by atomic structure, Danish physicist Niels Bohr published the first quantum theory of atomic structure. The theory wasn't perfect, but it did spur on the development of modern quantum theory. Bohr stated that electrons can only have certain orbits around the nucleus of an atom. He showed that the lowest-energy orbit would be closest to the nucleus. He also said electrons could jump from one orbit to another. They would jump to a higher orbit when they receive energy and, as they lose energy, they would jump back down, emitting light in the process (Figure 25). The color of the light depends on the difference in energy between the two orbits. It is the electron orbiting around the

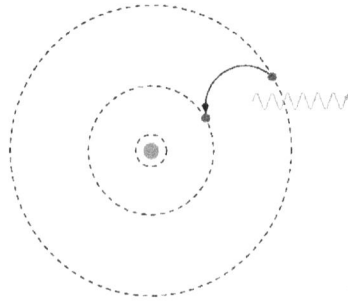

Figure 25 - Bohr's model of the atom showing the emission of a photon (signified by the wavy line) as an electron jumps down to a lower orbit (indicated by the arrow).

---

[70] http://cosmologyscience.com/cosblog/electron-is-not-a-fundamental-particle/

atomic nucleus which makes up the atom. Different numbers of different variations within the constructs of the atom determine what type of atom it is.

Interestingly enough, with something called the *"double slit experiment"* in 1961, Claus Jönsson discovered that a beam of electrons could behave as particles and as a wave, also known as *"wave-particle duality"*.[71] The really weird thing about this experiment is it shows that you can only determine the probability of the path a certain electron will take. If an attempt to measure the electron directly is made, it destroys the experiment and alters the results.[72]

That is part of the weird and interesting world of quantum mechanics. Due to measurement and observation, a particle can actually be altered. That brings us to possibly the strangest particle of all; the photon.

Photons

Photon particles come in a form we are all familiar with: that of light. We encounter photons every day of our lives, yet many times we are unaware of the miraculous beauty that surrounds such an astounding creation. While light is made of particles called photons, experiments also show beyond question that light is a wave. Light is so strange, in

---

[71]   http://physicsworld.com/cws/article/news/2013/mar/14/feynmans-double-slit-experiment-gets-a-makeover
[72] *The Quantum Universe*, Brian Cox and Jeff Forshaw, 21-25

fact, it has been theorized that light is actually a vibration from the fourth spatial dimension.[73]

This theory is especially intriguing when we consider the account of creation in the book of Genesis. We read...

1:3 And God said, Let there be light: and there was light.

4 And God saw the light, that it was good: and God divided the light from the darkness.

Genesis 1:3-4 (KJV)

It is possible this account is describing the moment photons came into physical existence. Sometimes it is interpreted as saying the light that came forth was the light of God, and in some ways that is true: in the sense that everything in existence comes from God. Yet, notice it says *"and there was light"*, implying that there was not *"light"* beforehand. Thus, this is most likely describing the light of our physical universe that comes in the form of photons, not necessarily the holy and eternal light emanating from God. To further support this idea, notice it says *"And God saw the light"*, also implying that there was not *"light"* to see beforehand. Clearly, all throughout the Bible, God is described as being radiant and full of light, yet this is not the same light being described here in Genesis. The light that is being described here is the physical light that was created by God. In essence, it is our normal, everyday, physical light created from the holy light of God Himself. Therefore, the idea that light is a vibration from a higher dimension might actually be

---

[73] *Hyperspace*, Michio Kaku, 8

accurate and, strangely enough, might be able to be supported using the Bible.

There is another extremely interesting quality of photons that not only exemplifies God's eternal nature and omnipotence, but also, in my humble opinion, shows a bit of His sense of humor. Einstein's Relativity (a topic we will get into further detail in a later chapter) shows that as you increase your speed, time actually slows down for you as compared to anyone else who isn't moving. It isn't just that a clock will run slower; it is biological as well. Your metabolism, brain synapses, breathing, heart rate, and everything else actually slows down. This effect of high speed is something that has actually been measured on a relatively small scale.

Einstein also showed that one cannot travel faster than the speed of light. As you travel faster and faster toward the speed of light, time literally goes slower and slower. If you could actually travel the speed of light (by far, a technological impossibility in our present age), time would literally stop.

Photons, which could be described as the carriers of light, exist at the speed of light. This means photons never *accelerate* to the speed of light. They exist exactly at the speed of light. The consequence of this is, from the photon's perspective, time does not exist.[74] This means that as soon as a photon is emitted from its source, even if it is a star millions of light years away, it immediately reaches its destination at that exact

---

[74] *Neil deGrasse Tyson on Photons and Relativity*, StarTalk Radio, Published March 14th, 2013 - http://youtu.be/5ELA3ReWQJY

moment. This, of course, is from the photon's perspective. From our perspective, we could look at a star a million light years away and deduce that it took the photons from that star a million years to reach our eyes. However, from the perspective of the photon, it was absolutely instantaneous.

The fact that time does not exist from a photon's perspective can be compared to God Himself existing outside of the bonds of time and space. Since time does not exist from the perspective of photons, they never change. It is impossible. It is the same with God.

Another interesting thing about photons is their ability to seemingly communicate with each other by means of something at an instant. Einstein called this *"spooky action at a distance"*, yet we would recognize it today as *"quantum entanglement"*. Somehow, by means that are not yet understood, photons seem to be able to communicate vast distances at faster-than-light speeds. This, of course, would seem to be theoretically impossible. It is no wonder Einstein was not a fan of this idea of quantum entanglement. However, by various means, it has shown to be true. Regardless of how far away they are from each other, photons seem to be able to communicate with each other instantaneously. To this day, how exactly this works is a complete mystery.

The thing that I find somewhat humorous about photons is how drastically different they are in reality than what we would normally perceive. The same could be said about God. We tend to see Him in certain ways but, many times, God doesn't fit into our idea of reality. God does seem to represent Himself in many ways throughout His creation. Much like His creation, the photon, God far surpasses all logic and reason. He is ultimately eternal and timeless.

Chapter 8

From the Smallest to the Largest

Lo, these are parts of his ways: but how little a portion is heard of him? but the thunder of his power who can understand?

Job 26:14 (KJV)

Strings and Branes

In the last chapter, we went through a few subatomic particles to show the basic building blocks of reality as we know it. Of course, any study such as this begs the question, *"What are subatomic particles made of?"* It seems everything must be made of something. If not, how could anything exist? We may also wonder where this leads. Atoms make up the Earth which is in the solar system which is in the Milky Way Galaxy which is in our universe; where does it end? Is there anything larger than our universe?

These are the questions we will address in this chapter. The simplest answer is *"nobody knows."* However, there are some very interesting ideas within the realm of physics that may help provide answers. We are going to be delving into the strange terrain of strings and branes. However, I will remind you, these ideas are theoretical at this point. There are some very specific mathematics to give these ideas credence, but that should not intimidate you.

Though these terrains are indeed strange, we are still talking about God's creation. Presented here is just an idea on how He might have gone about setting everything up. It would not surprise me if these things are proven as total nonsense someday, yet it also would not surprise me if these things are someday proven true.

All we can do for the time being is speculate and make educated hypotheses. Of course, the things discussed here go a bit beyond that, given there are solid mathematics to at least support these intriguing ideas. That being said, we can now explore the strange reality of the smallest and the largest: strings and branes. First, we should establish some of the history of physics that led to these ideas.

Unification

By now, the majority of us probably already know something about, or at least have heard the term, *"The Theory of Everything"*. This is the long-sought after theory that physicists recognize as their own holy grail. If anyone is able to discover a single unifying theory, that is, the theory of everything, they would surely win the Nobel Prize to say the least. This begs the question, what is it and why is it so important?

To answer this question, we must journey back to the time of Einstein and his general theory of relativity (Figure 26). With this theory of gravity, Einstein was able to show that space and time were much more malleable that originally thought. With the mathematics he

Figure 26 - Einstein and relativity (in this equation, R stands for relativity, i stands for intensity, k is for kelvin, and O is oxygen).

developed in this theory, Einstein set out to develop what is known as a *"unified field theory"*.

Einstein wanted to find one mathematical process that would describe all of nature's forces. So, instead of having a separate set of laws for each force, he wanted to discover a way to combine them into a cohesive whole. Einstein was unsuccessful in his pursuit, however he did provide a lot of groundwork that physicists still use today in order to accomplish the same ambitions.

At the time Einstein was on his quest for unification, the known forces were gravity and electromagnetism.[75] Einstein's goal was to develop a mathematical description that would bring these two forces together, in essence, unifying them. This was a monumental goal; one that Einstein was very serious about. He was so serious, in fact, that he dedicated the last thirty years of his life to it. Brian Greene explains…

"His personal secretary and gatekeeper, Helen Dukas, was with Einstein at the Princeton Hospital during his penultimate day, April 17, 1955. She recounts how Einstein, bedridden but feeling a little stronger, asked for the pages of equations on which he had been

---

[75] Gravity was described by Einstein's own theory of relativity while electromagnetism was described by James Clerk Maxwell through a series of equations showing the relationship between electricity and magnetism.

endlessly manipulating mathematical symbols in the fading hope that the unified field theory would materialize. Einstein didn't rise with the morning sun. His final scribblings shed no further light on unification. "[76]

When Einstein passed, the quest for a unification was quenched. At the time and up through the mid-1960s, most physicists were preoccupied with quantum mechanics and understanding the atom. To add insult to injury, it turned out that Einstein was only working on a piece of the problem. His work did not take into account two extra forces revealed by various experiments: the *"strong nuclear force"* and the *"weak nuclear force"*.[77] Unification would have to take these extra forces into account, meaning there would be the need to unify four forces, not only two.

Great strides to this end were made in the late 1960s and 1970s. It was already known that quantum field theory could be successfully applied to the electromagnetic force. Now, however, it was discovered it could also provide descriptions of the strong and weak nuclear forces. Finally, it was looking like the three nongravitational forces could be unified.

However, there was a problem. When physicists tried to apply quantum field theory to the force of gravity, the math would fall apart. General relativity and quantum mechanics were both incredibly

---

[76] *The Hidden Reality*, Brian Greene, 84-85
[77] The strong nuclear force is what holds together the atomic nuclei while the weak nuclear force is responsible for nuclear decay, as well as other things.

successful by their own right, the former for the large scale and the latter for the small, but they would not agree when mixed together. It would seem both would have to remain mutually exclusive.

Hope was restored in the mid-1980s with the new approach of *"superstring theory"*. It seemed there was finally a possibility that gravity could be included in a unified theory along with the quantum mechanics of the other three forces. Superstring theory (or *"string theory"* for short) took off at a fast pace. Mathematics were constructed, research was conducted, and a framework was built. However, there was still a lot unknown about string theory.

In the mid-1990s while trying to probe into the unknown, researchers found that string theory was intertwined with multiverse notions.[78] When researchers continued to refine the mathematics of string theory, they realized it was clearly shown that our universe could be a part of a multiverse. In fact, the math showed not only one type of multiverse possibility, but a variety of which we could be a part.

Quantum Fields

By some interpretations, classical physics describes a field as a sort of mist that fills a region of space and can contain disturbances in the form of ripples and waves.[79, 80] By Maxwell's interpretation, for instance, electromagnetic waves produced by a light source, such as a

---

[78] The term *"multiverse"* refers to the idea that there are multiple universes outside of our own. The collection of our universe along with these other proposed universes is known as the multiverse.

[79] Classical physics, such as that Isaac Newton taught.

[80] *The Hidden Reality,* Brian Greene, 87

light bulb, undulates across space to their destination. Maxwell showed the waves' movement by mathematics. An undulating field results in undulating numbers, meaning the numerical value of the field at any given location fluctuates between up and down repeatedly.

When quantum mechanics is used to define a field, the result is known as quantum field theory. Quantum field theory can be set apart from the rest by two distinct features. First, the value of a field at any given point will fluctuate randomly due to quantum uncertainty.[81] Second, that a field is composed of incredibly small particles, which are known as the field's quanta, a term we discussed in an earlier chapter.

For example, the electromagnetic field's quanta are photons. Quantum theory, building off of and slightly modifying Maxwell's classical interpretation, shows that the light bulb emits a stream of 100 billion billion photons every second.

Research of the past few decades shows that every field is subject to quantum fluctuations. Also, every field is associated with a type of particle. For example, electrons are quanta of the electron field and quarks are quanta of the quark field, so on and so forth. The mathematics of quantum field theory show these particles as points in space that possess no spatial extent or internal structure. The math is so sound, in fact, that not only is there no experimental data that counters its predictions, but it actually describes the behavior of particles with

---

[81] See also Heisenberg's Uncertainty Principle, developed by Werner Heisenberg in 1927, which states that the more precisely the position of a particle is determined, the less precisely its momentum can be known, and vice versa.

incredible accuracy. For example, the quantum field theory of electromagnetism, known as *"quantum electrodynamics"*, has calculations that match measurements to a precision of ten decimal places.[82] This is a truly astounding example of the precise agreement possible between theory and experiment.

As precise as quantum field theory can be, however, it fails to be able to include the force of gravity with the other three forces in a unified theory. Gravity is a different animal altogether. When the equations of general relativity are introduced into quantum theory, the math falls apart. When the mathematics are worked out, it is typical to get an answer of infinity. Of course, in certain areas this wouldn't be a problem. Some things could theoretically be infinite, such as the size of the universe. However, when trying to figure out probabilities, infinity is not a valid answer. By definition, the value of a probability has to be between 0 and 1 (or between 0 and 100 when considered in terms of percentages).[83] A probability of infinity is completely meaningless and shows there is a problem somewhere in the equations.

Physicists were able to determine the issue was due to the fluctuations of quantum uncertainty. By this time, mathematics were developed for the strong nuclear, weak nuclear, and electromagnetic fields. However, when the same mathematics were applied to the gravitational field, they fell apart. As it turned out, the fluctuations in the gravitational field were far more different and jarring. By comparison, if the fluctuations of the three nongravitational forces'

---

[82] *The Hidden Reality*, Brian Greene, page 88
[83] Ibid.

fields were equivalent to a person stomping around on the floor, the fluctuations of the gravitational field would be equivalent to an earthquake. This is due to the fact that the gravitational field is intertwined with the fabric of spacetime and its quantum fluctuations affect the entire structure.

For years, physicists largely ignored this problem because it only comes into play when considering extreme circumstances. Gravity really only makes its mark on massive things while quantum mechanics describe things incredibly small. The only time gravity and quantum mechanics come together in a noteworthy way is when something incredibly small, yet incredibly dense, is being considered. For example, when physicists consider black holes or the big bang, things that do involve enormous mass condensed down into a small space, the math breaks down. This leaves unanswered questions from a mathematical standpoint as to how the universe began and how it might possibly end.[84]

There are ways to calculate just how massive and how small a physical system would need to be for both gravity and quantum mechanics to play a noticeable role. The result actually turns out to be the Planck mass, which as we discussed earlier, is 2.17645×10^{-8} kg, or 10^{19} times the mass of a single proton, squeezed down to a volume of about 10^{-99}. This incredibly small volume could also be described as a sphere with the radius 10^{-33} (the Planck length). Due to this, quantum

---

[84] Keep in mind, this is from the standpoint that God is not involved whatsoever. Typically, our version of creation from Genesis and our version of eschatology from books like Daniel and Revelation would not be considered by physicists and mathematicians in working out these problems.

gravity is more than a million billion times beyond the scales that can be probed with even the most powerful particle accelerators technologically available today.

To add even more mystery, this unknown space between what we can observe and the Planck length could possibly be teeming with undiscovered fields and their respective particles. There could even be other things we have no concept of yet. Because of this it was assumed that to unify gravity and quantum mechanics, it would mean needing the capability to explore this expanse which, for the most part, is experimentally impossible at our current level of technological development. Most scientists concluded it was beyond reach and gave up the search for a single unifying theory. That is why, in the mid-1980s, there was a great deal of skepticism when word got out that there had been some major theoretical developments toward unification by means of a new approach: string theory.

String Theory

The basic idea of string theory isn't nearly as difficult to understand as is the math behind it.[85] Before string theory came along, it was widely assumed that the fundamental structure of nature was comprised of point particles with no internal structure and governed by

---

[85] The actual mathematical equations behind many things discussed throughout this book are far beyond what I personally can grasp, which is why I have chosen not to focus too much on those areas. However, mathematics aside, these ideas are still well within the reach of the average layperson, such as myself, so there is no need to allow the mathematical aspects to cause intimidation.

the equations of quantum field theory.[86] String theory redefined this assumption in some very interesting ways. Most notably, string theory suggests that particles are not merely dots. It is instead suggested that, at their core, they are unimaginably tiny, string-like filaments that vibrate (Figure 27). In essence, if you look deeply enough into any subatomic particle, you will find a string. Even more, string theory states that the strings within different particles are actually identical in nature but vibrate at different rates and in different

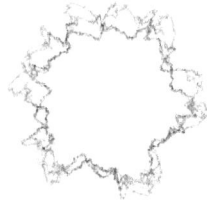

Figure 27 - According to string theory, it is tiny, vibrating strings that make up the fundamental reality of nature.

patterns. The vibrations of the string is what determines what type of particle it is to be. For example, an electron is less massive than a quark. According to string theory, the electron's string vibrates less than the quark's string (Figure 28).[87]

An analogy often used to describe this idea is that of the violin. The violin is a great comparison because, in reality, it contains an extraordinary amount of notes. Since a violin does not have frets, such as with a guitar, there is a variety of different vibrations that can be achieved between the musical notes in our classic scale. For example,

---

[86] See also what is known as *"The Standard Model"*: a theory that is commonly viewed as containing the fundamental set of particles (http://en.wikipedia.org/wiki/The_standard_model).

[87] This concept reflects the relationship between energy and mass that is described in Einstein's famous equation, $E=mc^2$ (energy equals mass times the speed of light squared).

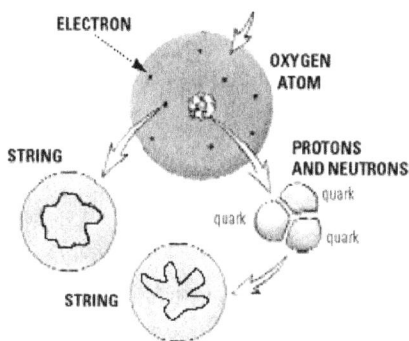

Figure 28 - Using the example of an oxygen atom, this shows the difference in vibration between an electron and a quark; a quark is more massive than an electron, so string theory states the quark's string would vibrate with more intensity than that of the electron.

you can play an A note, then play a B note. You can also play halfway in between those two notes to get an A# (A sharp), sometimes called a Bb (B flat). That is where the division ends within our classic scale of music theory.

However, with an instrument such as a violin, nothing is preventing you from playing a note halfway between an A and an A#. Theoretically, you could keep doing this until you get down to Planck length scales, and each note or vibration would be unique. This is the idea with string theory. Every unique particle contains a string that vibrates in just the right way for that particle to exist. All strings are the same; the only difference is their vibrational patterns.

In fact, the theory postulates that the vibrating string does not merely determine the properties of the particle that surrounds it, rather it *is* the particle. The string is incredibly miniscule, on the order of the Planck length. This essentially means strings are one-dimensional loops. Due to the string's incredibly small size, even today's most technologically advanced equipment cannot determine the string's structure. The Large Hadron Collider bombards particles together at energies beyond 10 trillion times that of a single proton at rest and can probe to scales of 10^{-19} cm, yet this is still not enough to accurately observe the Planck length.[88] Because of this, strings would still appear as dot-like if observed with even the most advanced particle accelerator in the world. Despite this, string theory states that particles are, in fact, strings.

There is much more that can be said about string theory, the content of which could easily fill multiple volumes of books. We will delve a bit deeper into some of these things in the next section. However, what has been presented thus far is sufficient enough to understand the next topic.

Branes

When string theory first came about, and for some time afterward, the idea of branes was largely ignored. As it turns out, however, branes and strings go hand in hand. String theory is no longer only a theory of one-dimensional strings, but is also a theory of branes that can extend in two, three, and even higher dimensions.

Branes (short for *"membranes"*) were introduced to the world of physics in 1995 when physicist Joe Polchinski of the Kalvi Institute for Theoretical Physics (KITP) in Santa Barbara established they were essential to string theory. Before this, there were propositions of brane-like objects by certain physicists. One example is what was known as a *"p-brane"* (I am sure the pun was intended in naming that one), an object that can extend infinitely far, but only in some dimensions.

---

[88] This is almost beyond comprehension. 10^{-19} cm is a millionth of a billionth the width of a single strand of human hair, yet this still is far removed from the Planck length.

Physicists were able to determine this by means of Einstein's theory of general relativity. There were also suggestions describing ways of confining particles to brane-like surfaces. However, the branes that Polchinski proposed were the first known type that could confine both forces and particles. As it turns out, lower-dimensional branes can theoretically trap particles and forces, even if the universe has many other dimensions. If string theory is accurate, then there is no getting around acknowledging the possible existence of branes.

Earlier in this book, we discussed how looking at lower dimensions can help put higher dimensions in perspective. We used the analogy of Flatland. We also realized how the two-dimensional Flatland would be just a slice of a three-dimensional world. We also suggested that our three spatial dimensions could be just a "slice" of a higher-dimensional reality. Branes can be understood in the same way.

In essence, a brane is a region of spacetime that permeates through a slice of space, which in itself could be multidimensional. The reason they are equated to membranes is because membranes are layers that either surround or extend through a substance. Branes can either be slices inside space or slices that surround space, much like a sandwich with the bread representing the brane and the lunchmeat representing space.

Now that physicists have had time to go over the theories and mathematics, they have come to the conclusion that the three dimensions of space in which we exist could be a three-dimensional slice of a higher-dimensional reality. They have even been able to define several characteristics of branes. For example, a brane would have to have fewer (or occasionally, the same number of) dimensions than the higher-dimensional space surrounding or bordering it. As long as this is maintained, branes can have any number of dimensions.

When considering a higher-dimensional reality, branes would be the boundaries of the full higher-dimensional space, or what is known as the *"bulk"* (Figure 29). The bulk and branes are completely different things. The bulk extends in all directions and spans all dimensions. Because of this, the bulk is recognized as "bulky" while branes are flat (by comparison and only in some dimensions). If a brane borders the bulk, some of the bulk's dimensions would be parallel to the brane while others would lead off of it.

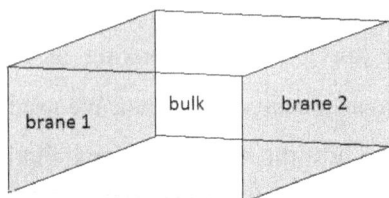

Figure 29 - Branes can exist as boundaries between higher-dimensional space, also known as the bulk.

When something such as a particle reaches a boundary brane, it bounces back. This is known as *"reflective boundary condition"*. The interesting thing is energy is not lost nor does the particle get absorbed into the brane. The brane is the end and nothing gets beyond it. The boundary brane is the end of dimensional existence.

Branes also have the characteristic of trapping things on lower-dimensional surfaces. It conveys the idea that, in a reality with extra dimensions, not all matter is able to travel everywhere. Particles or strings can actually be confined to a three-dimensional brane within a higher-dimensional reality. Brane-bound objects lack the ability to travel through extra dimensions that extend off of the brane due to physical laws. Not every particle would have to be bound to the brane; some might be free to venture out into higher dimensions. However, regardless if the brane in question is slack and can move or is taut and sits still, the particles that are bound never leave; they cannot become "unstuck".

As stated before, branes and the bulk could have any number of dimensions as long as the brane has less dimensions than the bulk. The number of dimensions that a brane-confined particle can move around in is what is known as the *"dimensionality of a brane"*. The easiest to consider is that of three spatial dimensions because that is what is most relatable to us as three-dimensional beings.

The universe could have many dimensions. However, if the particles and forces are trapped on a brane that extends in three dimensions, they would still behave as if they only occupied three dimensions of space. Particles and forces that are trapped on a brane can only move along that brane's dimensions.

The truly interesting thing is, as mentioned before, there are things that physicists know can never be trapped on a brane. Gravity is one of those things. According to Einstein's general relativity, gravity is woven into the framework of space and time. This means that gravity must be able to extend through every dimension of space and time. General relativity would have no meaning if gravity could be confined to a brane.

This idea could very well lead to an answer to the gravity problem in unification. It could help explain why gravity is so weak and vastly different compared to the other forces. If the other forces, along with the rest of the universe, are bound to a brain yet gravity is free to roam the bulk, we should expect gravity to be weaker and different. This is an idea physicist Lisa Randall proposes in great detail in her book *Warped Passages.*

Now that we have a basic understanding of branes, we can integrate strings and discover how they tie in. As stated earlier, with modern string theory, branes must be considered. Gone are the days when you could have one without the other.

The Integration of Strings and Branes

In 1989, a type of brane, known as the D-brane, was discovered in the equations of string theory by Jin Dai, Rob Leigh, and Joe Pulchinski. String theory shows that strings can either be closed loops or open-ended. For string theory to work, the string's open ends would have to go somewhere. The only location that string theory allows for the open ends of strings to be is on the D-brane (Figure 30).[89] Since the bulk can contain more than one brane, not all open strings have to end on the same brane (Figure 31). String theory tells us how many dimensions these branes would have. As stated before, branes can conceivably extend into any number of dimensions. Typically, in string theory, the way branes are labelled is to use the number of spatial

---

[89] The "D" in D-brane is named after Peter Dirichlet, a German mathematician who lived in the nineteenth century.

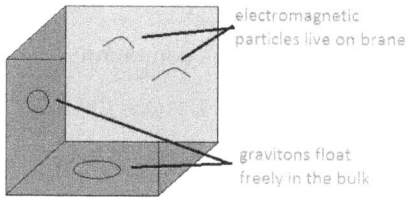

electromagnetic
particles live on brane

gravitons float
freely in the bulk

Figure 30 - This shows how open strings, such as with electromagnetic particles, remain attached to a brane while open strings are free to travel the bulk.

dimensions (not temporal) in which they extend. For example, a brane that extends in three dimensions would be called a 3-brane.

This idea of open and closed strings is what makes branes so important to string theory. Gravity is thought of being in the form of a closed string that makes up the graviton particle. Since the string is closed, this would allow gravity freedom to travel through the bulk while the rest of the forces, being open strings and connected to the brane, would not possess that freedom (Figure 32). This could

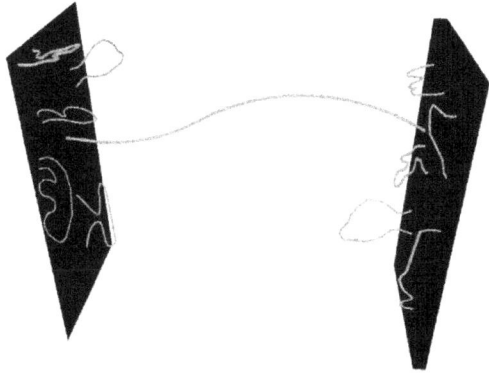

Figure 31 - This is an example of a string that has two ends attached to different branes.

be the answer to why gravity is so much weaker than the other three forces. There is also the possibility that this could lead to a single, unifying theory of all four forces. You just simply cannot have strings without branes.

Before 1995, five versions of string theory existed. Each version included different forces and interactions. Then in 1995, at a conference at the University of Southern California, theoretical physicist Edward

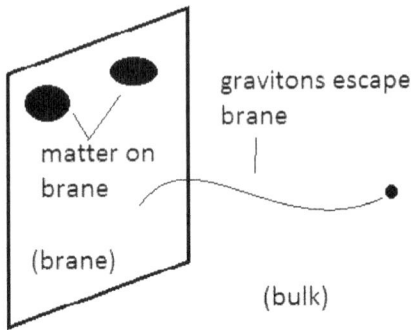

gravitons escape brane

matter on brane

(brane)

(bulk)

Figure 32 - This shows how gravity can escape into the bulk while ordinary matter cannot. This is what defines the difference between closed strings and open strings.

Witten shocked the string theory community by showing various dualities in the five versions.[90] In essence, Witten showed that each of the five versions were looking at different aspects of the same issue. With the added understanding of branes, the five apparently different theories were shown to be the same theory from different vantage points, all of which were valid and true. Witten named this new theory *"M-theory"*.[91]

There is still a lot unknown in M-theory. No one yet knows the best way to express and formulate M-theory, but most string theorists recognize this as their primary goal. M-theory offers a lot of potential within the physics world. It could give a more unified picture of string theory's potential as a theory of quantum gravity.

While many of the things within this chapter and throughout this book might seem strange and impossible on the surface, we have to remember that God, the ultimate Creator, is not bound by our

---

[90] In particle physics and string theory, a duality describes when two theories are actually the same theory with different descriptions.

[91] Interestingly enough, to this day, Witten has not revealed what the meaning of the *"M"* in M-theory stands for. Some theorize it might stand for *"magic"*, *"mystic"*, or might even represent the first letter of Witten's last name, only upside-down.

presuppositions. Imagine how strange it would have sounded the first time people heard Galileo postulate that Earth, in fact, revolves around the sun and not the other way around. We might think of that as slightly humorous today, but if these theories of strings and branes prove to be true in the future, we could easily find ourselves falling in the same trap as Galileo's detractors if we aren't careful. I do agree it is always good to maintain a healthy amount of skepticism, but I think Proverbs 18:13 states it best when it says...

> *He that answereth a matter before he heareth it, it is folly and shame unto him.*

We should at least hear these things out and consider the possibilities.

The Continuous Spoken Word of Creation

There is one last thing to consider concerning string theory. There is an interpretation of Hebrews 11:3 that states God not only spoke everything into existence, but that He is *still* in the process of that spoken and creative word. The idea is, since God is outside of time, His spoken word is eternal and is holding reality together from the beginning to the end of time as we know it. Hebrews 11:3 states...

> *"Through faith we understand that the worlds were framed by the word of God, so that things which are seen were not made of things which do appear."*

This is a particularly interesting concept concerning string theory. If string theory ever proves to be true, it could be that the vibrations from the string are actually caused by higher-dimensional sound waves from the eternal voice of God. Of course, I write "sound waves" for lack of better term. This idea is speculative, however it is definitely interesting to consider.

Chapter 9

The Mysteries of Time and Entropy

Declaring the end from the beginning, and from ancient times the things that are not yet done, saying, My counsel shall stand, and I will do all my pleasure:

Isaiah 46:10 (KJV)

The Art of Defining Time

Time can be tricky to define. It may not seem so on the surface, but how often have we really thought about an adequate definition of time? Most of us have probably never found ourselves in a situation where we needed one. Time is something we all live with. Time is always with us. We have never been without it. Time is something we all share in together. It is something we all know, even if its definition is something we have trouble putting into words.

Some might say time is simply the ticking of a clock. That is certainly one way of looking at it. We schedule our entire day, every day, by the moving of the hands of a clock. Those hands tell us when to wake up, when to eat, when to go out and make money, when to meet a friend, and when to go back to sleep. We live our lives by the collection of gears hanging on the wall, but is that *time* or just a means of measuring it? Time existed before we had mechanical clocks to measure it. Time would continue to exist even if there was no intelligent life available to measure it via things like the sun, moon, and stars. Clocks are a great help in our society, but what exactly are they measuring? The website Dictionary.com defines "time" as the following...

> *"the system of those sequential relations that any event has to any other, as past, present, or future; indefinite and continuous duration regarded as that in which event succeed one another."*[92]

That is certainly a mouthful. While that definition is accurate, it seems there should be a more concise way of saying it.

Some would define time as the progression of change. This is probably the most accurate and easy to understand definition. With every passing second, there are substantial changes throughout the universe; galaxies are churning, stars are burning, and planets are rotating. Even on our own planet and in a less expansive scale, things are always changing. When we think something is still and completely as rest, it is only a clever illusion. Air molecules are shifting around, electrons are orbiting atomic nuclei, and photons are firing off in every direction. Our reality is truly one of change.

That is what makes the Planck time we discussed earlier so interesting in how it is measured. Nothing is faster than the speed of light. Nothing is shorter than the Planck length. There is no other change

---

[92] http://dictionary.reference.com/browse/time?s=t

that is possible within the time it takes light to travel the Planck length. Due to this, we truly do exist in sections of time rather than the illusion of smooth progression to which we are all accustomed. Just the thought of that is truly astounding.

Viewing time as a measurement of change certainly helps get our heads around the issue, but it isn't complete. For example, if there is more change in one second than in another, time doesn't speed up or slow down. Time may *feel* slower if I sit and stare at a wall as opposed to writing this book; however, an hour is still exactly an hour in duration. Perhaps St. Augustine said it best when he said...

"What is time? If no one asks me, I know. If I wish to explain it to one that asketh, I know not."[93]

Probably the only entity that has the capability to define and experience time perfectly is God Himself. The reason for this is He is the only being truly outside of time. Some might think of angelic entities as being outside of time as well, but remember, angels had a beginning. They were created. The very fact that they have a beginning prohibits them from existing outside of time.[94] There is only one truly eternal being in existence: God Almighty.

---

[93] *Confessions*, St. Augustine

[94] That being said, I don't know how time actually works in the spiritual world. There is reason to believe it would work the same as in our physical reality, such as the fact that time is the same within the first three dimensions, however this does not prove the same applies for higher dimensions. I also do not know if angels have the ability to travel through time. There are good reasons for both sides of the argument. The only one we know who is truly not bound by time whatsoever is God.

Of course, that is not to say God doesn't insert Himself into time here and there. Clearly He does. However, we must keep in mind that time is still His creation and He is not bound by it. Think of this in terms of a house. When you build a house, you are building a place to be inhabited. When it's finished, you are free to enter and exit at will. You are not bound by the house you built. Much is the same for God and time.

While we move through time in sections called Planck time according to quantum physics, we tend to see time in larger blocks we can fathom. Depending on what we're doing or describing, things can happen within five minutes, or ten minutes, or an hour, or a day, so on and so forth. This is all just personal perspective determined by what we are trying to describe. The reality is, at least from God's perspective, the past is as real as the present and the present is as real as the future.

In philosophy, this is called the *"block time"* or *"block universe"* perspective. Instead of thinking that time is something we move through or that moves around us, space and time is viewed as a single block of spacetime. Of course, there are different opinions to this approach. St. Augustine, the fifth-century theologian and Church Father, actually wrote about time from his own perspective. In Book IX of *Confessions*, he wrote...

"What is by now evident and clear is that neither future nor past exist, and it is inexact language to speak of three times – past, present, and future. Perhaps it would be exact to say: there are three times, a present of things past, a present of things present, a present of things to come. In the soul there are these three aspects of time,

and I do not see them anywhere else. The present considering the past is memory, the present considering the present is immediate awareness, the present considering the future is expectation."

St. Augustine, of course, was speaking from a human and physical perspective. This way of looking at time is known as *"presentism"*; that is to say, only the present truly exists. From our human perspective, this would be accurate. However, as stated before, from God's perspective, the past, present, and future all exist equally.

Strangely enough, physics actually agrees with this view. In the world of physics, the past, present, and future all exist as equally real. This is called *"eternalism"*. The only thing that separates the past from the future is the present, which is determined by what is known as the *"arrow of time"*. Just as a car can drive north or south, the arrow of time, theoretically and purely from a physics point of view, could have ended up pointing forward or backward in time. It just so happens to be pointing toward the future from the past.

The Arrow of Time

It is interesting to consider the arrow of time. It points the same way for all of us all of the time. We never really give it much thought. When anything happens by means of cause and effect, the mere fact that it happens in the same progression every time becomes a constant reminder that the arrow of time is pointing in the correct direction. It never spontaneously points the other way. A classic example is that you can turn an egg into an omelet, but you can't turn an omelet into an egg. At the very least, it would be exceedingly difficult to do so and would require quantum technology far beyond the limit of what we have today.

Another example often given is that of coffee. You can mix milk into coffee, but removing the milk once it is mixed is a far more dreadful task. The arrow of time is affixed in a certain direction and it doesn't change. It is a fact of nature. But why should this be so? Why don't things ever go backward, even for just a moment?

As it turns out, the answer lies in the idea of what is known as *"entropy"*. Comparable to things like temperature or energy, entropy communicates the state of a system. Entropy measures how disorderly a system is. A classic example often used in physics to illustrate this point is a stack of papers on a desk. If the papers are neatly stacked and orderly, it has low entropy. If the same papers are then scattered haphazardly around the room, it is an example of high entropy. Coffee and milk in separate containers have low entropy, but milk mixed into coffee has high entropy. Entropy rises when something moves from order to disorder.

Entropy ties in with time as part of the measuring process. We know, due to Einstein, that time and space are woven together into spacetime. But when we think about it, time and space are drastically different. Mainly, directions in space are equal, yet directions in time (i.e. past and future) are vastly different. Imagine if you are floating in space where there is no real up and down; every direction is equal with every other direction. Time, however, is never like that. We live in the present, we can reconstruct the past with memories or left over evidence, and the best we can do for the future is made educated predictions that may or may not prove accurate. There is far more certainty in the past than there is in the future. There is no equality concerning the directions of time.

CHAPTER 9

The word used in the physics world to describe equality, such as among the directions in space, is *"symmetry"*. Spatial direction is symmetric. Temporal direction, however, is asymmetric, meaning there is no equality. If we look at ourselves in the mirror, we still recognize ourselves. Nothing too fantastic would stick out due to the reversal. This is due to symmetry. However, something quite different happens with time. If we try and reverse time, everything moves backwards and looks completely unnatural. It would be like trying to watch a movie in reverse. It would be obvious there was a problem.

This means the arrow of time is not a result of the underlying laws of physics, at least as far as physicists are concerned.[95] They typically consider the direction of the arrow of time as a temporal consequence of the birth of the universe. As physicist Sean Carroll states...

> *"The beginning of our observable universe, the hot dense state known as the Big Bang, had a very low entropy. The influence of that event orients us in time, just as the presence of the Earth orients us in space."*[96]

Personally, as a Christian before anything else, I find it easier and far more satisfactory to recognize that there was very little to no entropy when God created the universe. Whether this creative act came in the form of a hyper-inflated Big Bang type of event or not is beside the point. Whatever it looked like, God's creation was *"very good"* in the

---

[95] *From Eternity to Here: The Quest for the Ultimate Theory of Time*, Sean Carroll, page 31
[96] Ibid., 32

beginning, yet many things changed after the fall.[97] However, before we can fully examine how entropy came into existence, we need to further define what is meant by entropy.

Entropy

The characteristics of entropy are probably most accurately explained in the Second Law of Thermodynamics:

The entropy of an isolated system either remains constant or increases with time.

This law is incredibly reliable.[98] In fact, scientists sometimes point out that the Second Law of Thermodynamics is the most dependable of all the laws of physics.

We really owe our modern understanding of entropy to Austrian physicist Ludwig Boltzmann. In 1877, Boltzmann first proposed his ideas and definition that we use today. However, the concept of entropy and its relationship to the Second Law of Thermodynamics goes back to German physicist Rudolf Clausius in 1865. The Second Law of Thermodynamics itself goes back even further to a French military engineer in 1824 by the name of Nicolas Léonard Sadi Carnot. It is amazing how Clausius could use entropy in the Second Law of Thermodynamics without having access to Boltzmann's definition and

---

[97] Genesis 1:31 (also Genesis 1:4, 10, 12, 18, 21, and 25 for mentions of creation being *"good"*)

[98] The First Law of Thermodynamics states that energy is conserved.

Carnot was able to formulate the Second Law of Thermodynamics without including entropy.

Interestingly enough, the nineteenth century was big for the science of thermodynamics.[99] The main goal at the time was to build more advanced steam engines. The people involved in thermodynamics would study things such as energy, pressure, and temperature toward this end. This actually led us right into the industrial age.

We know today that the temperature of something is the measure of the kinetic energy of its atoms and that energy is translated into heat.[100] However, in 1800, science was not advanced enough to understand energy quite that well, or even believe in the existence of atoms for that matter. Carnot was driven by trying to find out how efficient an engine could be. He wanted to know how much useful work he could get from a given amount of fuel. He discovered there was, in fact, a limit. Carnot discovered that the production of waste heat needed to be minimized in order to maximize efficiency. Given this, he realized that there is no perfect model for an engine. Even the most advanced and efficient engine would lose some energy along the way. That is how he came to the conclusion that the operation of a steam engine is a completely irreversible process. This basically meant that steam engines did something that could not be undone.

In 1850, Clausius realized Carnot's discovery was an example of a law of nature. He postulated this new law as *"heat does not*

---

[99] Thermodynamics is the study of heat and its properties.
[100] Kinetic energy is the energy of motion.

spontaneously flow from cold bodies to warm ones." Think of an ice cube in a glass of water. As the ice melts, the water gets cooler. The opposite never happens. Nature tends toward the side of what is known as *"equilibrium"*, meaning everything eventually evens out to be as uniform as possible. By realizing this as a law of nature, Clausius was able to redefine Carnot's conclusions concerning steam engines.

At first, it might seem like the idea of heat not flowing from cold bodies to warm bodies has nothing to do with the Second Law of Thermodynamics, but in fact, they are essentially the same law. In 1865, Clausius reformed his expression of this law of nature by adding entropy, which was a new concept at the time. He showed that the tendency of nature toward equilibrium is the same as stating the entropy of a closed system would only increase and never decrease. When equilibrium is reached, maximum entropy is also reached.

One way to look at entropy is as a measurement of the usefulness of a certain amount of energy.[101] When you put gas in your car, that gas has a certain amount of useful energy. As your car runs, that energy is used and put to work. Throughout the process, the energy becomes increasingly useless as it turns to heat and motion. As the energy loses its usefulness, entropy increases.

There is a way for entropy to decrease according to the Second Law of Thermodynamics, but it comes at a cost. As it turns out, we can decrease the entropy of one thing, but in the process we would have to create even more entropy somewhere else. For example, we could build

---

[101] *From Eternity to Here*, Sean Carroll, 34

a machine to reassemble omelet atoms back into an egg, or separate milk from coffee, but the energy required for these machines would be excessive, thereby creating entropy elsewhere.

There is a difference between open and closed systems that determines what entropy can do. Open systems, meaning objects or processes that interact with the outside environment on a large scale to exchange energy and entropy, allow for entropy to decrease only if entropy is created elsewhere. In closed systems, meaning objects and processes that are removed from external influences, entropy will always increase until equilibrium is reached, in which case it will remain constant.

Boltzmann picked up where Carnot and Clausius left off in understanding entropy (Figure 33). Carnot and Clausius lived in a time without specific knowledge of atoms. Boltzmann was able to come up with a more atomic understanding of entropy. He realized that we look at things macroscopically, that is to say, on the large scale. If a few atoms where moved around in our morning coffee, we would never notice. It wouldn't change the temperature, consistency, or taste of the coffee. It would still have the same energetic potential it had beforehand.

Figure 33 - Ludwig Boltzmann's grave is located in Zentralfriedhof, Vienna. The equation inscribed ($S = k \log W$) is the formula of entropy in regards to the number of ways the microscopic components of a system can be rearranged without changing its overall appearance on a macroscopic scale. S represents entropy, k represents a constant (aptly named Boltzmann's Constant), log is the natural logarithm, and W represents the number of ways a system can be changed.

Boltzmann also realized there was a limit to this. Objects with low entropy, such as an egg, are more delicate in regards to rearranging atoms. We could exchange some of the egg's shell atoms for the yolk atoms, but it wouldn't take very long of doing that for us to begin to notice. Objects with low entropy are more sensitive to atomic rearrangement while objects with high entropy are more versatile. Basically speaking, Boltzmann took Clausius and Carnot's idea of entropy and reintroduced it in terms of atoms.

It was because of Boltzmann that the idea of entropy really began to make sense. He introduced the idea that entropy tends to increase in an isolated system because, quite simply, there are more ways to be high entropy than to be low entropy. For example, think back to our first coffee analogy. There is an astronomical number of ways that milk molecules and coffee molecules can be mixed together to produce the same essential result. However, to separate them again, there are far less. The milk molecules have to be with all the other milk molecules and same with the coffee.

In terms of physics and probability, there is a slight chance that when you mix milk into coffee, if you mixed it long enough, the molecules would just collect in perfect order and completely separated. However, the chances are astronomical and you would have to stir the coffee for billions of years to reach that result. Thus, there are more ways, making it is far easier, to have high entropy from low entropy rather than the other way around.

Now that we have more of a complete view of entropy, we can look at the theological ideas surrounding it. There are different ways of looking at this, but basically the main idea is that entropy entered the world when Adam fell from grace. The fall of mankind brought something into the world that didn't exist before: death and decay.

We aren't given very much information as to the specifics of creation before the fall. We would assume that everything was perfect since a perfect God created it all and sin had not yet been introduced. But does this have to mean there was no entropy whatsoever? Not necessarily. Remember, entropy measures the usefulness of energy. It could be that entropy was just incredibly low in the beginning. After all, stars would have still been burning and photons would have still been emitted and absorbed into the earth. Also, Adam and Eve were created as beings who ate food (Genesis 2:16). Unless they ate food for pure enjoyment, it would seem they needed to consume food to be converted into energy for their bodies. If they needed to replenish their fuel source, this would mean they would lose energy, the amount of which would depend on how active they were. This could be looked at as an expression of entropy.

Given this, perhaps it isn't that the initial creation was absent of entropy. Perhaps entropy was just incredibly low. Perhaps the entrance of sin and death made entropy into something it was never meant to be. Instead of a tame kind of thing, it may have turned into a twisted, super-charged form of itself, into the version of it we have today. This is all, of course, highly speculative. At the very least, it gives us something to consider about the initial conditions of creation itself.

Time Travel

Our study so far brings us to a very interesting question: is there a way to reverse entropy without creating even more entropy elsewhere? There are a few theoretical answers to this question, but it really all boils down to one point. With the current direction of the arrow of time, entropy cannot be decreased. It would seem the only way to reverse entropy would be to travel back to a time when entropy was lower. But can such a thing be done? Is time travel a feasible possibility? If so, are there ethical and theological problems to consider? Of course, in writing a chapter such as this, discussion about potential time travel cannot be avoided. Because this topic is so vast, I thought it best to consult an expert.

Interview with Dr. Ronald Mallett

For help in sorting out the possibilities, I contacted Dr. Ronald L. Mallett (Figure 34), a physicist and fellow believer, for an interview regarding some of his research into the issue of time travel.

Figure 34 - Dr. Ronald Mallett is a theoretical physicist, academic, and author of the book Time Traveler: A Scientist's Personal Mission to Make Time Travel a Reality. He has been a professor at the University of Connecticut since 1975. Dr. Mallet is most known for his research into time travel.

* * *

This interview was transcribed by Deeanna Williams from a recording of a phone call, then later edited by Josh Peck. Only minor grammatical corrections have been made. A special thanks goes to Deeanna for her exemplary work.

CHAPTER 9

JOSH PECK: How did you become interested in the study of time?

DR. MALLETT: The reason I became interested in time travel had to do with a tragedy that happened in my family during my early life. I was ten years old and my father was really the center of my life. I was the oldest of four children. I grew up in the Bronx, New York and my father was a television repairman. He was very good at what he did and he looked like he was very healthy. Even though he worked very hard, he had time for the family. He spent a lot of time answering questions and he gave me toys like a gyroscope and crystal radio set. As I said, I really adored him. We didn't know he had a weak heart and he died completely suddenly of a massive heart attack. He was only thirty-three years old. It really shook my world. I mean, it really turned my world upside-down. I went from being a happy kid to a rather depressed kid. I should mention that after he died, the family plunged into poverty. It was a very difficult time and I don't know how my mother survived it. I think it was her religious faith that helped her to survive.

About a year after he died, I came across a book that changed my life. It was called *The Time Machine* by H.G. Wells. It was actually what was known as a Classics Illustrated version of it. The book, right at the very beginning, said that scientific people know very well that time is just a kind of space and that we can move forward and backward in time just as we can in space. When I read that, I knew that this was the thing that could save me. This would be my lifeline because I thought if I could build a time machine, I could go back and see my father again. I could tell him what was going to happen and be with him, but maybe I could figure out some way to prevent it from happening. That became my mission. It was actually a secret mission because, even at the age of eleven, I knew people were already worried about me, so I didn't tell people what I was interested in doing. That was the beginning.

About a year after that, when I was twelve, I came across the second book that changed my life. As I mentioned, we were quite poor after my father died, and I had this very serious book habit. I had to read. The only books I could afford were at the Salvation Army. You could pick up paperbacks for about five cents. One time, when I went in there, I saw the cover of this paperback. It had a picture of Einstein on it and next to Einstein it had an hourglass. I didn't know what Einstein did, but I knew he was this great genius. Incidentally, as a side note, Einstein died in the same year as my father, in 1955. That's always been an interesting coincidence. Even though I didn't understand, the cover of the book told me there must be a relationship between Einstein and time because it had Einstein next to an hourglass. So I bought the book and even though I couldn't understand everything that was in it, I did get the gist of it. It said Einstein said that time was not something that was absolute. In the ordinary classical physics of Newton, you can't do anything to change time, but according to Einstein, you can change time. I knew that if I could understand Einstein, then that would be the key. I remember the book. I still remember the name of it. It was called *The Universe and Dr. Einstein* by a man name named Lincoln Barnett. That was the beginning of my desire to understand Einstein.

It didn't just go simply from A to Z; that is to say, I didn't just simply go from that to graduating and going to college. In fact, we were too poor for me to go to college, so after I got out of high school, I joined the Air Force. I was enlisted during the Vietnam War period. I used the GI bill when I got out to go to Penn State. That's where I made my specialty in Einstein's work; in special and general relativity. I eventually understood that Einstein had developed two theories. One theory was called the special theory of relativity which he developed in 1905. That theory, in a nutshell, says that time can be changed by motion. That is to say, the faster an object moves, the more time will slow down for that object. Time for a moving clock will actually slow down. That's essentially the essence of Einstein's special theory of relativity. It turns out that there are experiments that have been done that actually show that time can be slowed down. In fact, one that most people don't know about was done in 1971 at the Naval Observatory. What they did was take two atomic clocks; one of the clocks was kept at rest at the Naval Observatory and the other was put on a moving plane. The plane was travelling close to the speed of sound, and when they brought the plane back, they found that the clock that had been on the plane had actually slowed down. Now, it was only by fractions of a second, but it did show exactly what Einstein predicted. Time slows down. The effect becomes greater the faster you move. The closer to the speed of light, it's not just in terms of fractions of seconds, but in terms of hours. In fact, there's a device called the Large Hadron Collider at CERN in Geneva, Switzerland. They have subatomic particles that they can accelerate close to the speed of light. Some of these particles normally only live for a millionth of a second. What they can do is, by accelerating these particles close to the speed of light, they cause these particles to live ten times longer than they normally would.

Remember too, when I'm talking about a clock, I'm not talking about a mechanical mechanism. Your heart is a clock. That means your heart would slow down. You would actually age less than other people. This means if you were travelling fast enough, for you time might only be a few years, but if you were moving fast enough, decades could be passing for everyone else. You could wind up literally in the future only being a few years older whereas here on Earth, decades have passed. So that's essentially time travel into the future. One way of altering time is by altering speed, but that just carries you into the future. Of course, I was interested in going into the past, and that turns out not to be possible in the special theory of relativity, no matter how fast you go. Number 1, you can't go faster than the speed of light, and Number 2 you can't travel back into the past, no matter how fast you go.

It turned out about ten years after that, Einstein developed the second theory. That was called the general theory of relativity. This theory has to do with the fact that gravity can affect time. That's the essence of it. That is to say that Einstein was able to show this mathematically. I should mention that when I use the phrase "Einstein showed", I mean Einstein used mathematical equations to show these things. Einstein didn't do the experiments. Those experiments were done later by experimental physicists. Einstein was a theoretical physicist. Einstein was able to show that the stronger gravity is, the more time would slow down. For example, gravity here at the surface of the Earth is stronger than in high altitude, so clocks should actually should run slower here at the surface of the Earth than they do at high altitudes.

Once again, that's also been shown experimentally. In fact, the most dramatic manifestation of that, in terms of a device that nearly everyone has in their car, I certain do, is a GPS. The GPS unit in your car has a clock in it. Right now, about 12,000 miles above us, there are 24 satellites in geosynchronous orbit, meaning they are in certain places over the Earth at any given time. The satellites have clocks in them. The way a GPS system works is that at a certain time, the signal will send from one of these satellites, actually three of these satellites, to your unit. If you know the time the signal was sent and the time it was received by your unit, and you know the speed of the signal is the speed of light, then you can compute distance. So that's the way in which your unit works. Unfortunately, when the system was set up, it wasn't working right. It was giving incorrect locations. The reason for that was the fact that they had forgotten to take into account Einstein's theory of gravity, which says that the clock in your unit is actually running slower than the clocks on board the satellites. That means that the clocks were getting out of sync. They actually had to use Einstein's theory and use computers to take into account that difference in which time was moving for the clocks. That actually corrected the problem. That is to say, by taking into account the fact that clocks in the satellites are running faster than the clocks in the unit, they were able to correct it, and that's why it works now. So we do know time is affected by gravity. That turns out to be the key also, eventually, to time travel to the past.

JOSH PECK: How would your proposed idea for a time machine work?

DR. MALLETT: As I said, my work is actually connected with Einstein's general theory of relativity which has to do with time being effected by gravity. It turns out that my work involves the fact that in the normal classical physics, the only thing that can create gravity is matter. For example, the earth creates a gravitational field which keeps us anchored. The sun creates a gravitational field that keeps the earth in orbit and so on. The thing is, in Einstein's theory, not only can matter create gravity, but light can create gravity as well. The breakthrough of my work was to realize that if gravity can effect time and light can create gravity, then light can effect time. In other words you could actually use light of a particular type to effect gravity.

It turns out that the type of light you have to use is a laser because it can be focused to a narrow beam. What I realized is that this laser can actually create a gravitational field that can alter time. I should mention, once again like Einstein, I am a theoretical physicist. What I did was to use equations. Essentially my work is based on Einstein's gravitational equations. What I did was solve those equations for a particular type of light. I was able to show you

CHAPTER 9

need a circulating light beam, and you can create a circulating light beam in a number of different ways. You can actually have light bounce off of mirrors. That is one way of creating a circulating light beam. It turns out that if you have a circulating light beam you can create a particular type of gravitational field that can actually cause a twisting of space and time.

Formally time travels and formally all of us move along a time line from the past to the present to the future. It is a linear line that goes from our birth to our death along that line. However, if we can twist time into a loop, then we can actually twist that time line in such a way that we can go from the past to the present to the future, since we have made the time line into a loop, then we can go from the future back into the past. So by using a circulating light beam, what I was able to do was show that you can create a twisting gravitational field. Essentially you can twist time into a loop, and along that loop of time you can go back to the past. So that is essentially what my device does. When I say that, once again, all of this is based on mathematical equations I have solved that shows this.

The thing is, just as in the case of Einstein's earlier theories, experiments have to be done. But, in physics, experiments are extremely expensive. People don't realize that. They see these things in movies and they think that is the way things work in real life. One of my favorite movies is *Back to the Future*, but real life is nothing like that. You cannot go into your garage and create anything that has to do with real physics. The type of experiments that are going to be needed, just the startup cost for the type of work that I am doing, is going to be about a quarter of a million dollars. And that is cheap by the way. I should mention, the Large Hadron Collider that I was mentioning earlier, its whole purpose is just accelerating sub-atomic particles. That experiment cost them ten billion dollars. These experiments are extremely expensive at the stage that we are at right now. I have an experimental partner who is a specialist in lasers and we are at the stage of trying to get the funding that is necessary to do the experiments. It's a challenge to try to get the funding, but the physics is solid. The equations say that by using circulating light beams, you can twist space and eventually you can twist time. If you can twist time, then you can travel backwards into the past. So you might say, to use an analogy with the movie business; having a script is one thing, getting the movie made is another. So, right now, we are at the stage of having the script and trying to get the funding to get the movie. That's where we are at.

JOSH PECK: Do you have any kind of timeline on how close you might be to developing an experimental prototype?

DR. MALLETT: When you say a timeline, that is no pun intended. No, it depends on funding. If we get the funding, then I will be able to develop a timeline. There is no timeline without having the funding. It would be like, using the movie analogy, if I have the script and then you would say "how long is it going to take you to make the movie?", well, I can't make the movie until I get the money to make the movie. So having the script is necessary but it is not sufficient. I have the equations and the physics there, but until we get the funding it is not possible to talk about a timeline. Now I could say, suppose we got the adequate funding, it would probably take, just in the initial phases, about five years to develop the first basic aspect to show that we can twist space by bending light. To twist time is going to require many, many millions of dollars beyond that. Suppose that we got all the funding that we need, you're probably talking around the order of ten years if we got all the funding. But we don't have anywhere near the funding so there is no timeline.

JOSH PECK: How could communication between two points in time work with your idea for this machine?

DR. MALLET: What you could do is send information back, and I should mention that the work that I am doing, we are not trying to send people back in time. We are looking at trying to show that we can send subatomic particles and information back. In some ways, sending information back is more important than sending people back. You are in the information age by the way. In fact, people have asked me, "What would be one of the uses that you would have?" and one of the uses for me would be as an early warning system. Imagine if you had a way of sending information back to the past that could warn you of things like tsunamis, earth quakes, hurricanes...the thousands of lives you could save. A way in which you could send the information back would be by using sub-atomic particles.

You could use neutrons to send information back. A neutron spins like a little top and it only has two particular directions that it can spin. It can spin up or it can spin down. You could assign a one to the spin up direction and you could assign a zero to the spin down direction. If you had a beam of neutrons, for instance, that would spin up, spin up, spin down, that would be one, one, with zeroes....that is binary code. So by using the spin of neutrons, it would be binary code to send the information back. In the past you would have to have a device there to decode the spins to tell you so that you could translate the information into information that we could use. That would be the way in which you would do it.

JOSH PECK: What are some of the paradoxes that might come up in sending messages back in time?

DR. MALLETT: One of the main paradoxes that may come up is what is known as the "Grandfather Paradox", and usually people grasp that in terms of sending people back. Suppose you went back in time and somehow prevented your grandparents from meeting each other. To prevent your grandparents from meeting each other, they don't have your parents and if they don't have your parents, then your parents don't have you. So how did you go back? Since you would cease to exist, how would you go back to prevent your grandparents from meeting each other? That is called the "Grandfather Paradox", where you do something that essentially seems as though you could erase your own existence. So, that is a serious problem as far as going back into the past. You don't have that problem if you are going into the future, but you do have that problem if you are going back into the past.

However, it turns out that physics itself says there might be a way out of that particular paradox and this has to do with what is known as Quantum Physics. The relativity is only one of the pillars of modern physics; the other pillar in modern physics is Quantum Mechanics. It has to do with how matter and energy behave; how the atom essentially behaves. Quantum Mechanics underlies all the more modern technology. Our PC's, our cell phones, all of these things depend on Quantum Mechanics. In fact, our whole understanding of the elements in the Periodic Table depend on our understanding of Quantum Mechanics. Quantum Mechanics does not predict certainties, unlike classical physics where you could actually make definite certain predictions. In Quantum Mechanics, you could talk about the probability of something happening.

This leads to some interesting facts. Quantum Mechanics, in fact, leads to a whole new notion called the "parallel universe". The idea behind a parallel universe has to do with something that was dealt by a physicist, Hugh Everett, back in 1957 at Princeton. He wanted to apply Quantum Mechanics to the universe as a whole. What he found as a result was the fact that there is a possibility of two outcomes to an event. What can happen is that both outcomes can occur but in different universes. Let me give you a simple example that I use and I actually mention this in my book. Suppose that today you were trying to decide between having a fish sandwich and a cheeseburger. The moment that you chose the fish sandwich, there would be a split in the universe. You would now be a Josh Peck in a separate universe that has chosen the cheeseburger. So the you in the universe that chose the fish sandwich is separate from the you that chose a cheeseburger. You are both real but they are now in two separate universes. This happens for every single possible decision that you and everyone else makes. If there is more than one outcome, then both outcomes occur, but they occur in different universes. That is mind boggling because that means there is an infinite number of these parallel universes that are branching off all the time. And it doesn't have to do with human consciousness, it is something in which the way the world works.

In other words, if an electron has the possibility of taking one path or another, it takes both paths but in separate universes. This is called the "Parallel Universe Notion", where all of these outcomes are occurring but in different universes. It was a physicist named David Deutsch who applied this to time travel. What he found was that, when you go back into the past, as soon as you arrive in the past there is this split, and you arrive in a parallel universe. In that universe you actually could prevent your grandparents from meeting each other. You would just now find yourself locked into this strange universe in which you never were born and you would still be there. However, remember I said there was a split and in the other universe, you don't arrive in that universe when you get to the past. That universe is the one that leads to you.

In other words, since you don't arrive in that universe, your grandparents meet each other, have your parents, and eventually your parents have you. So, what the upshot is it says that time travel to the past is possible, but the past you arrive in is not the past you came from. So, there is no paradox. That is one of the ways in which physicists, and I'm one, believe the Grandfather Paradox may be resolved. But that is only one possibility; there are others.

One of the other ones is the fact, when you go back in the past, you can't really alter the past. Whatever you try to do in the past will prevent you from actually altering it. The simplest example would be, suppose you are determined that you are going to prevent you grandparents from meeting each other. When you arrive in the past, you break your leg, so you can't go and do that. That is a very simple example of that. The point is that, essentially with this other alternative, it says when you try and go back into the past, something happens to prevent you from altering the past.

Those are the possibilities but which one actually occurs? We don't know. We won't know until we actually do the experiment. It may turn out that we do, in some way, really alter the past, and the past that we think we are living is a past that is actually, even though it seems real to us, is actually a past that has been tampered with through time travel. Like I said, we won't know until we actually do the experiment. Which one? The parallel universe is one of the favorite ones as far as a boundless notion of a paradox.

JOSH PECK: Do you have any concerns that this technology could be misused in some way?

DR. MALLETT: Oh, of course. I mean, the thing is however, and this is important, is the fact that any technology can be misused. One simple example that I like to use is one that actually was mentioned to me by my step-son during a conversation we were having with other people. What he did was pick up a butter knife and he said, "This is technology, and I can use this to butter my bread, but someone could also use this knife to stab someone." That is technology, so are we going to ban butter knives?

So we have to realize that whatever we create has both positive and negative possibilities associated with it. It is up to us and that is why we have laws that regulate things. Air travel is something that is very much regulated and it is going to be the same when it comes to time travel. It's going to happen, but we are going to have to make sure it is regulated. That is why it is important for people to realize that these possibilities are out there so they can begin to think about them. How are we going to deal with it? Because, we are going to have to deal with it. This is another thing that is frustrating for me is the fact that, unfortunately, in this country we have a tendency to do things in a reactionary way. What I mean by that is the fact that we do things technologically sometimes because we are afraid of it being done by someone else. The simplest example of that is Sputnik. We had the technology to send a satellite into space long before the Russians did. However, it wasn't until they sent the satellite into space that all of a sudden we were in a space race. Let's suppose the CIA tomorrow uncovered the fact that North Korea was doing research on time travel. I would have more funding than I would know what to do with.

The thing is, we shouldn't wait to see what's going to happen somewhere else before we decide to actually look at these things ourselves and start thinking about how we are going to have to deal with it. But yes, there is a possibility of misuse. But, that is not going to stop the technology just simply because of the fact that we don't want it because it is possible that it has negative connotations to it. What we are going to have to do is say okay, how are we going to regulate this and how are we going to make the maximum use of this for the good?

JOSH PECK: Let's say you got all the funding you needed and were able to build a working machine; is it possible, once you turn on the machine, messages from the future will immediately start presenting themselves?

DR. MALLETT: Not necessarily, because the thing is, you have to remember that things can't just simply happen. You have to have a receiver and that receiver has to be tuned into whatever it is you expect to get. Remember I said, for example, that coded messages could be sent back in binary code using neutron spins. That would mean, what you would have to do is set up your device. It would have to have detectors that were set up to receive the specific type of information that you were planning on sending from the future. So, your experiment would have to be designed with the future possibility in mind of what it is that you are sending back. So, you're not going to get anything unless you have designed the experiment to receive something that you are specifically going to design for a later date to send information back. Do you see what I am saying?

JOSH PECK: Absolutely. So, if you had the machine, the detectors, and everything running, and let's say you wanted to send a message back; if I understand this right, you can only go back as far as the machine detectors have been turned on, is that correct?

DR. MALLETT: Correct. The first type of experiments that we would do aren't going to be as dramatic as getting a message; something like Alexander Graham Bell got when they set up the telephone. What it will be is something involving the sub-atomic particles that I mentioned before, that can only live for a very short period of time and then they completely disintegrate. What we would do is send a beam of those particles into the region where we believe we have twisted time. Now, normally some of these particles are going to get whipped around and they are going to live longer than they normally would. That's an effect we would expect to see if they are traveling fast. But now, some of those particles that go back in time, if they go back just a little bit and come forward those particles will actually live less than they normally would. We would actually get a distribution by sending in a set of identical particles that decay within a certain time normally. We see a distribution in which some of these particles are living longer than they should and some of those particles are living shorter than they should. The ones that are living shorter than they should would actually show us that these particles have been sent into the past. That is the way in which we would first look at it.

JOSH PECK: It sounds like, even with a working prototype, we are still quite a ways away from being able to send actual messages back.

DR. MALLETT: Yes. Then, once again, this is real physics and it would be in stages, but that would be the way in which we would initially know we actually have sent something back; even just a little bit. Once we have been able to do that a little bit, then we will be able to bootstrap that, and that will allow us to be able to eventually design something much more sophisticated.

That is the way in which it happens in physics. If you read about the history of the laser, it is a great example. The public doesn't generally realize this, but Einstein actually developed the theoretical equations for the possibility of a laser back in 1917. It wasn't until the 60s that technology caught up. It was very, very difficult to produce a laser; extremely difficult. But, once they were able to produce the simplest laser, then all of a sudden things exploded. We actually then realized that we could get practically anything to lase. So, that's the sort of thing that happens with technology. Once you're able to do it even for the simplest case, then what happens is there is an explosion of understanding, and then the development of it increases exponentially. But, as I said, we are a long way from that because of the fact that we have baby steps associated with it.

JOSH PECK: I have a couple of hypothetical situations concerning time travel and the many worlds interpretation that I'm curious to get your opinion on. It seems to me, and correct me if I'm wrong, that whether or not you receive messages before actually sending them might provide evidence for or against the many worlds interpretation. For example, let's say you turn the machine on and leave it alone for a week. Then you decide to send a message back in time one week; to the time you turned the machine on. Now, if there is only our one universe, then it would seem once you send a message back, you would remember receiving the message a week ago. In essence, the original timeline when you received no message would be erased and replaced with a timeline in which you had. In that instance, there would be some evidence of the success of the machine. You would have no recollection of turning the machine on and receiving no message. For you, you would have turned on the machine and immediately received a message, so there would be direct evidence the machine does in fact work.

Now, if there are parallel universes, the message would get sent back one week and you would receive it, yet that would branch off into a new universe. But where does that leave you in the original universe? From your original perspective, you would send a message back, it would disappear, and absolutely nothing would have changed. It would seem that if you turn on the machine and start receiving messages, it would provide evidence contrary to many worlds. However, if you turn it on and receive nothing immediately, it might provide evidence supporting many worlds. So my question is, if the many worlds interpretation is correct; you send back a message that creates a branch to a parallel universe; how would you ever be able to know the machine had in fact worked and not just displaced the message somewhere else or destroyed it altogether?

DR. MALLETT: Well, there is going to be an uncertainty about that. When you turn on the machine and you have it set up so that it could detect things and it detects something, let's suppose the message that it detects says, in essence, "A week from now you're going to send particles back." That is the message that you got. Now, let's suppose that a week from now, you are perverse and say "I'm not going to send anything back", how is it that I got something back there? Well the thing is, it could be that would actually be saying that there is probably a parallel universe, because you got something, you see? If you do send it, then that actually could tell you this is the universe that I sent it from. It is my own universe. So in a sense, if you get something and you decide not to send something then that could be evidence of a parallel universe. If you get something and you do decide to send something then that could be evidence of the fact that you actually did it within your own universe.

JOSH PECK: One of the more attractive things about the possibility to send messages back is something you touched on earlier. It would seem this type of technology could be used to prevent tragedies; for example, 9/11. This is a bit similar to the first hypothetical, but let's say your machine existed at the time of 9/11. 9/11 happens and you send a message back to prevent it. Let's say they receive it in the past and are actually able to prevent it. It seems this could lead to one of two outcomes; either preventing it causes a branch to another universe, in which case we would still be living in the universe in which 9/11 happened, essentially preventing nothing in our own universe, or it would change the past in our own universe, therefore creating a reality in which the message would never be sent back in the first place; no 9/11, no message, and with no message comes no prevention, in which case we would be back where we started from, in a timeline in which 9/11 is our reality. So my question is, are these limitations valid, and if so, is there any way around them to actually be able to change the past in a way we all can experience?

DR. MALLETT: It would simply mean that reality is much more plastic than we thought, because we actually really did change our universe. So the universe that sent this back, our universe, actually no longer exists. In other words, the universe now that you think you're living in really isn't as solid as you think it is. That is a scarier possibility, but that's a possibility.

JOSH PECK: It would seem, even if there were limitations, at least it could be used to save lives during natural disasters, like you pointed out. For instance, we can't prevent a hurricane, even if we knew about it ahead of time. But, we could warn people and save lives. So, either way, the hurricane is going to happen so there will always be a reason to send back the message. Unless many worlds is true and we send something back yet don't get to experience the changes, there is at least one way we can use a machine like this to improve things in a tangible way. What are some other applications for a machine like the one you propose?

DR. MALLETT: Well, one of the things that I mentioned in my book, which is really fairly far out but not so far out as one might think, is the fact that it is very likely there are now what physicists and astrophysicists call extra solar planets. These are actually planets that are orbiting other suns. It wasn't known until the 90s; it had been speculated that these might exist but it wasn't known until the 90s that there could actually be other solar systems like ours. It turns out that is highly likely, not only is it likely. We have seen other systems. It turns out that some of these planets are too close to their suns to inhabit any kind of life and some of them are too far away. They might have an exotic form of life, but it would be very strange. But, there are some planets that are just in the right zone. In fact, the name of these planets have been given by physicists which gives you an indication of the nature of the planet, is "Goldilocks" planets.

In other words, these are the planets that are just right. Some of them may support life forms that are very much more advanced than ours and that have been there for very much longer than we have, and so it turns out that they may have developed time travel much earlier than we have. If we encounter these civilizations eventually, we could use their devices which have the same limitations, but suppose they had turned on their devices ten thousand years ago. When we find these, we could visit our distant past as well, using their technology. The thing is, to me, it would be exciting because it would open up all our distant past to see history. I can't even imagine what it would be like to actually be able to see ancient Egypt and ancient Rome.

So, to me, visiting the past just to see what the past was really like would be one of the other really exciting things, but it won't be possible with our type of terrestrial technology because, right now, we haven't invented it. But, as I said, once again, even though it sounds a bit far out it's not beyond the possibility that eventually we will encounter extraterrestrial civilizations. This doesn't have anything to do with UFOs, by the way. Extraterrestrial civilizations would actually have had time travel and we could use it to visit our ancient past. So, it's not beyond the realm of possibility that our distant past may eventually become open to us when we develop the space technology that is necessary to travel to other planets.

JOSH PECK: That, for me, could easily go into another whole line of questioning, but I won't do that to you. You mentioned that you wrote a book entitled *Time Traveler*. Can you tell me about what readers can expect to find in your book?

DR. MALLETT: Definitely. What I decided was to write a book that was not just going to be your typical popular science book. There are plenty of those out there. What I wanted to do was something that would be interesting as a story. So, the book is actually a combination of memoire and popular science book. It actually follows my development, but it also follows my understanding of relativity and everything so that people who are reading the book will actually gain an understanding to learn a story; the story of my development, why I became interested, and my father. There is an interesting story there, but woven within that story is my increased understanding of relativity and Quantum Physics. So, people will actually grow and learn as I grow and learn in the book.

First, we will start out with a rudimentary understanding. Then it gets more and more sophisticated, but it never goes into something beyond the popular science level. That is what people can expect. They can expect a blend of memoire and popular science which will talk about all of the things that they have heard about; wormholes, cosmic strings, and black holes. I talk about other people's work as far as time travel is concerned; how they use wormholes as possible time machines and cosmic strings. It covers all of these things, but it does it at a popular level. But, as I said, it is embedded in a story. That is one of the reasons why the award winning film maker Spike Lee became interested in it. He has actually bought the rights for this earlier and he has written a script for a feature film. It is going to be an actual feature film, like the ones in theaters, about my story and my work, and it is for that reason. Incidentally, if you ever get the chance, one of the other programs that I think you and your wife would really enjoy, in fact it's the one that made my work come to Spike Lee's attention, is *This American Life*. They had a radio program a few years ago which they focused on my work. It was called *My Brilliant Plan*. It is considered to be one of their most popular episodes of *This American Life*. You might like to hear that some time. That is what people can expect in the book, a memoire plus popular science that talks about the real possibility of time travel.

JOSH PECK: Is there a release date set or a timeline when people could expect to see the movie?

DR. MALLETT: That is the reason why I used that earlier example for you of having the script, then getting the movie made. What has to happen is, the studio now has to pick up the option on the script, and that requires getting the money to make the film. So, right now, it is just at the script stage. But that, in itself, is an advance but still not in the stage of being made into a film yet without the budget.

JOSH PECK: If people want to know more about you and your work or order your book, where can they go?

DR. MALLETT: Oh yes, the best place as far as if people were interested in getting the book, I would recommend Amazon.com paperback because it is very inexpensive. As far as learning about my work, they can go to the University of Connecticut website, which is www.uconn.edu. Go there and they can find me. The other way, if they wish, is to also contact me via Facebook. In other words if they just put in a Facebook friend request, I will be happy to add them to my Facebook.

* * *

A very special thanks goes out to Dr. Mallett for providing this informative and extensive interview.

Chapter 10

Higher than Higher-Dimensional Creation

In the beginning was the Word, and the Word was with God, and the Word was God. The same was in the beginning with God. All things were made by him; and without him was not any thing made that was made.

John 1:1-3 (KJV)

The Last Leg

Throughout this book, we have dealt with many ideas concerning the creation from a scientific lens, science from a biblical lens, and the Bible from a Christian lens. We have described what makes up three-dimensional physical reality and speculated about the fourth spatial dimension. We discussed dimensions higher than the fourth spatial and even dealt with some of the entities that could be residing there. By now, you might be asking yourself the obvious question: where is all of this leading?

In these last two chapters, we are going to be describing the nature of everything above creation and higher-dimensional reality. This last leg of our journey will focus on discovering some rather obscure, yet immensely impactful and important, attributes of the Creator Himself. We are also going to see how He has created all of us with the same obscure attribute, or at the very least, the potential for them.

How Many YHWHs?

Most likely, all Christians reading this book are familiar with the idea of the Holy Trinity; the idea of God existing as a separate-yet-equal, three-yet-one entity in the form of Father (YHWH), Son (Jesus), and Holy Spirit. It seems, many times, this doctrine is taught from a primarily New Testament approach. Certainly, there are plenty of places in the New Testament that proclaim the truths of the Trinity. However, there is just as much, if not more, that can be learned from the Old Testament concerning the Trinitarian nature of God.

Deuteronomy 6:4 tells us that there is one Lord (translated from the sacred name of God, YHWH). He possesses many qualities that set Him apart from any other entity in existence. First and probably most obvious is that He created everything and everyone in existence, physical and spiritual. Apart from that, He can call out the end from the beginning and the beginning from the end, an idea we dealt with in an earlier chapter. He can also insert Himself into time and space more than once during any given instant. This is where the idea of an Old Testament Trinity comes in.

The first time I was confronted with this, it was quite a shock. It came in the form of a verse I read many times, but often glossed over. Because of this, I missed the full scope of what was being said. This idea was first presented to me in a description of the destruction of Sodom and Gomorrah:

Then the Lord rained upon Sodom and upon Gomorrah brimstone and fire from the Lord out of heaven;

Genesis 19:24 (KJV)

Both times, when the word "Lord" is used, it was translated from the Hebrew "YHWH". Both instances are certainly referring to the same Person. The first YHWH is raining the fire and brimstone and the second YHWH is supplying the fire and brimstone. Both are the same Person, yet they are playing two different roles. Some have referred to this as the Pre-incarnate Jesus while others say that Jesus is the incarnated YHWH. I believe what we have here is another example of a duality. Both conclusions are looking at the issue from different angles, yet both are correct. We can show this further by looking at some other examples.

Sometimes, this idea can be picked up in the language YHWH uses to refer to Himself. For example:

I have overthrown some of you, as God overthrew Sodom and Gomorrah, and ye were as a firebrand plucked out of the burning: yet have ye not returned unto me, saith the Lord.

Amos 4:11 (KJV)

Notice the language used here. The end of the verse tells us who is talking with *"saith the Lord"*. This whole verse is spoken by YHWH. He starts off referring to Himself as *"I"* at the beginning of the verse, but then switches to third person language as He points back to when *"God overthrew Sodom and Gomorrah"*. YHWH is confirming the idea that He exists as more-than-one of Himself. They are both YHWH, yet there is only one YHWH.

If this is difficult to wrap your mind around, don't worry, you are not alone. This is the nature of God we are trying to describe. We are not going to be able to fully understand YHWH's nature since His ways are higher than our ways and His thoughts are higher than our thoughts (Isaiah 55:9).

The Angel

This second manifestation of YHWH comes through in the Bible by a variety of descriptions. One of the most common is *"the angel of the Lord"*. Before we start looking at examples, I would like to clarify one point. In the past and even in the present, there have been odd methods implemented to define this angel apart from all other angels. Sometimes it is said that if the Bible states *the* angel of the Lord, it is talking about the Pre-incarnate Jesus, whereas if it states *an* angel of the Lord, it is referring to a normal angel. In my humble opinion, I don't believe the issue is entirely black and white. I believe it all has to do with context of the passage in question. There are times, such as in the resurrection account found within the gospels, when *an* angel could still be referring to a manifestation of one of the Persons of the Trinity.[102]

A good example of the relationship between God and the angel of the Lord can be found in the book of Genesis concerning the story of Abraham. First, to set the scene:

---

[102] For more information on this, refer to my Ministudy book *Sorting Out the Resurrection and Ascensions of Christ*, which is also contained in my compilation book, *Ministudy Anthology 1*. Both books are available at www.ministudyministry.com.

CHAPTER 10

^{22:1} And it came to pass after these things, that God did tempt Abraham, and said unto him, Abraham: and he said, Behold, here I am.

² And he said, Take now thy son, thine only son Isaac, whom thou lovest, and get thee into the land of Moriah; and offer him there for a burnt offering upon one of the mountains which I will tell thee of.

Genesis 22:1-2 (KJV)

Here we get the introduction of the story. Since the majority of readers are probably already familiar with this account, we do not need to study the entire passage. However, we do see something interesting once we skip down a few verses:

^{22:11} And the angel of the Lord called unto him out of heaven, and said, Abraham, Abraham: and he said, Here am I.

¹² And he said, Lay not thine hand upon the lad, neither do thou any thing unto him: for now I know that thou fearest God, seeing thou hast not withheld thy son, thine only son from me.

Genesis 22:11-12 (KJV)

This one is a bit more subtle than the first one we looked at concerning the destruction of Sodom and Gomorrah. In the beginning of verse 11, we are told that the angel of the Lord is speaking. This seems to flow nicely until after the angel states *"I know that thou fearest God"*. The next thing the angel says is *"thou hast not withheld thy son, thine only son from me"*. The last word *"me"* doesn't seem to fit with the rest of the passage. Back in verse 1, we learned that is was God Himself who required this from Abraham. Therefore, it was God who Abraham wasn't withholding his son from. However, in verse 12, it seems as though the angel is taking credit. The reason for this is that the angel *is* God. The angel is a manifestation of, for lack of better term, the "second YHWH".[103]

Another great example of this is found in the account of Moses and the burning bush in chapter 3 of Exodus:

> *3:1 Now Moses kept the flock of Jethro his father in law, the priest of Midian: and he led the flock to the backside of the desert, and came to the mountain of God, even to Horeb.*
>
> *2 And the angel of the Lord appeared unto him in a flame of fire out of the midst of a bush: and he looked, and, behold, the bush burned with fire, and the bush was not consumed.*
>
> *3 And Moses said, I will now turn aside, and see this great sight, why the bush is not burnt.*
>
> *4 And when the Lord saw that he turned aside to see, God called unto him out of the midst of the bush, and said, Moses, Moses. And he said, Here am I.*
>
> *Exodus 3:1-4 (KJV)*

Verse 2 tells us that the angel of the Lord appeared to Moses in a flame of fire from the middle of the bush. Moses then decides to turn around

---

[103] Keep in mind, we are not talking about two separate beings or gods here; we are talking about the dual (and really Trinitarian) nature of one God, the only God, YHWH.

to take a closer look. As he does so, the Lord starts talking to him. So, who is in the bush, the angel or the Lord? The answer is both, yet both are one. Both are the one and only YHWH.

We have seen two examples of how the angel of the Lord is actually the Lord YHWH Himself. We can also connect the angel of the Lord to Jesus Christ, thereby showing that Jesus is the physical incarnation of YHWH.[104] We only need to look at a few comparative passages that tell the same idea concerning one biblical account, yet in profoundly different ways.

First, consider a passage where God is giving specific instructions for entering the Promised Land.

[23:20] Behold, I send an Angel before thee, to keep thee in the way, and to bring thee into the place which I have prepared.

[21] Beware of him, and obey his voice, provoke him not; for he will not pardon your transgressions: for my name is in him.

[22] But if thou shalt indeed obey his voice, and do all that I speak; then I will be an enemy unto thine enemies, and an adversary unto thine adversaries.

Exodus 23:20-22 (KJV)

Again, notice the odd language YHWH uses. He first says that He is going to send His angel. In verse 21, He warns to not provoke the angel because *"he will not pardon your transgressions: for my name is in*

---

[104] As is often said, Jesus was "fully God and fully man".

him". Keep in mind, He doesn't say that the angel can't pardon transgressions; the idea is that the angel chooses not to. It says the angel *"will not"*. It does not say the angel *"cannot"*. This is how we know this angel is the second YHWH. Only YHWH can forgive sins. In verse 22, YHWH again uses some very interesting grammar. He says *"if thou shalt indeed obey his voice, and do all that I speak"*. If you obey *his* voice and do all *I* speak…this is very peculiar indeed. The angel of the Lord and YHWH are the same being, yet somehow separate.

We have just read that it was the angel of the Lord who brought the children of Israel to the Promised Land in the last passage. Now consider this comparative passage:

4:35 Unto thee it was shewed, that thou mightest know that the Lord he is God; there is none else beside him.

36 Out of heaven he made thee to hear his voice, that he might instruct thee: and upon earth he shewed thee his great fire; and thou heardest his words out of the midst of the fire.

37 And because he loved thy fathers, therefore he chose their seed after them, and brought thee out in his sight with his mighty power out of Egypt;

38 To drive out nations from before thee greater and mightier than thou art, to bring thee in, to give thee their land for an inheritance, as it is this day.

Deuteronomy 4:35-38 (KJV)

This passage first reinforces the position that the Lord is God and there is none else beside Him. We then find out that God Himself is claiming to be the one who led the Children of Israel to the Promised Land. This further shows the complex relationship between the angel of the Lord and the Lord. They are one in the same, yet different.

To further complicate the matter, consider another comparative passage:

> *2:1 And an angel of the Lord came up from Gilgal to Bochim, and said, I made you to go up out of Egypt, and have brought you unto the land which I sware unto your fathers; and I said, I will never break my covenant with you.*

> *2 And ye shall make no league with the inhabitants of this land; ye shall throw down their altars: but ye have not obeyed my voice: why have ye done this?*

> *3 Wherefore I also said, I will not drive them out from before you; but they shall be as thorns in your sides, and their gods shall be a snare unto you.*

> *4 And it came to pass, when the angel of the Lord spake these words unto all the children of Israel, that the people lifted up their voice, and wept.*

> *5 And they called the name of that place Bochim: and they sacrificed there unto the Lord.*

> *Judges 2:1-5 (KJV)*

What is really interesting is verse 1 says *an* angel of the Lord and not *the* angel. This shows what I mentioned before; there is no perfect formula for identifying the speaker when it concerns *an* or *the* angel of the Lord. We need to take it in context. Sometimes *an* angel of the Lord is the same as *the* angel of the Lord. What is also interesting is this angel of the Lord is making the same claims as God in the previous passage. *The* angel of the Lord is *an* angel of the Lord and is *the* Lord Himself. Of course, this can be confusing, but it also shows us how impossibly far above us God really is.

By now you might be asking yourself, how does Jesus tie into all of this? As if this weren't already complicated enough, the answer to that question comes through in yet another comparative passage:

> *1:4 For there are certain men crept in unawares, who were before of old ordained to this condemnation, ungodly men, turning the grace of our God into lasciviousness, and denying the only Lord God, and our Lord Jesus Christ.*
>
> *5 I will therefore put you in remembrance, though ye once knew this, how that the Lord, having saved the people out of the land of Egypt, afterward destroyed them that believed not.*
>
> *Jude 1:4-5 (KJV)*

By looking at the original Greek, we can determine that the *"Lord"* spoken of in verse 5 is Jesus Christ. We know this because the word for *"Lord"* in verse 5 is the same word for *"Lord"* in verse 4 when referencing Jesus. It is a different Greek word used altogether than that which is used for *"Lord God"* in verse 4.[105] Therefore, according to Jude, it was Jesus Christ who saved the people out of Egypt. We have the angel of the Lord, an angel of the Lord, the Lord, and Jesus Christ all claiming responsibility of this one event. Every single one of them is correct because, as we well know, we serve only one God. Again, remember the Trinity. Our singular God can be more than one while remaining singular.

The Name

As we saw in the previous example, YHWH said He put His *"name"* in the angel. What is meant by this? Are we to assume the literal name of the angel was YHWH, or is there something else going on here? Again, we need to consider the context. When God establishes His name in a certain place, it means His essence is there. Consider this passage:

> *But unto the place which the Lord your God shall choose out of all your tribes to put his name there, even unto his habitation shall ye seek, and thither thou shalt come:*

> *Deuteronomy 12:5 (KJV)*

It should be fairly obvious that this is not referring to the literal name "YHWH" or the four Hebrew letters that make up the Tetragrammaton: Yod, Hey, Vav, and Hey. To show this, we can skip down a few verses:

---

[105] "Jude 1 (KJV)." Blue Letter Bible. Accessed 31 May, 2014. http://www.blueletterbible.org/Bible.cfm?b=Jud&c=1&p=0&rl=0&ss=1&t=KJV

Then there shall be a place which the Lord your God shall choose to cause his name to dwell there; thither shall ye bring all that I command you; your burnt offerings, and your sacrifices, your tithes, and the heave offering of your hand, and all your choice vows which ye vow unto the Lord:

Deuteronomy 12:11 (KJV)

We can see here that the name mentioned is the presence of YHWH Himself. We know this by the phrase *"cause his name to dwell there"* and is further supported by mention of the offerings, sacrifices, and tithes. God doesn't require anybody to bow down and worship four Hebrew letters; we are required to worship God Himself.

The Lord hear thee in the day of trouble; the name of the God of Jacob defend thee;

Psalm 20:1 (KJV)

In this passage, we see how the name of God can actually defend. YHWH hears you in your day of trouble, and YHWH will defend you.

And David arose, and went with all the people that were with him from Baale of Judah, to bring up from thence the ark of God, whose name is called by the name of the Lord of hosts that dwelleth between the cherubims.

2 Samuel 6:2 (KJV)

Here is another passage showing that the name is not referring to the Tetragrammaton. This verse tells us that the name of the ark is called by the name of the Lord that dwells between the cherubim. Note that it says *"called by"* and not just *"called"*. It is not called the name of the Lord. It is called by the name of the Lord. Furthermore, there is no biblical description of the Tetragrammaton ever being engraved in the ark. What is described, however, is that YHWH Himself was present on the ark between the cherubim.

> *Behold, the name of the Lord cometh from far, burning with his anger, and the burden thereof is heavy: his lips are full of indignation, and his tongue as a devouring fire:*

> *Isaiah 30:27 (KJV)*

This passage makes this point extremely clear. The name of the Lord is actually personified. We learn that the name of the Lord bears the same type of description that the Lord does many times throughout the Bible. We have the same thing happening with the name as we did with the angel. They are both YHWH, but are type of second YHWH, equal and the same yet separate and different.

There are times when the Bible just comes right out and tells us the presence of the Lord and the angel are both YHWH. Consider this passage:

> [6:11] *And there came an angel of the Lord, and sat under an oak which was in Ophrah, that pertained unto Joash the Abiezrite: and his son Gideon threshed wheat by the winepress, to hide it from the Midianites.*

> [12] *And the angel of the Lord appeared unto him, and said unto him, The Lord is with thee, thou mighty man of valour.*

[13] And Gideon said unto him, Oh my Lord, if the Lord be with us, why then is all this befallen us? and where be all his miracles which our fathers told us of, saying, Did not the Lord bring us up from Egypt? but now the Lord hath forsaken us, and delivered us into the hands of the Midianites.

[14] And the Lord looked upon him, and said, Go in this thy might, and thou shalt save Israel from the hand of the Midianites: have not I sent thee?

[15] And he said unto him, Oh my Lord, wherewith shall I save Israel? behold, my family is poor in Manasseh, and I am the least in my father's house.

[16] And the Lord said unto him, Surely I will be with thee, and thou shalt smite the Midianites as one man.

[17] And he said unto him, If now I have found grace in thy sight, then shew me a sign that thou talkest with me.

[18] Depart not hence, I pray thee, until I come unto thee, and bring forth my present, and set it before thee. And he said, I will tarry until thou come again.

[19] And Gideon went in, and made ready a kid, and unleavened cakes of an ephah of flour: the flesh he put in a basket, and he put the broth in a pot, and brought it out unto him under the oak, and presented it.

^{20} *And the angel of God said unto him, Take the flesh and the unleavened cakes, and lay them upon this rock, and pour out the broth. And he did so.*

^{21} *Then the angel of the Lord put forth the end of the staff that was in his hand, and touched the flesh and the unleavened cakes; and there rose up fire out of the rock, and consumed the flesh and the unleavened cakes. Then the angel of the Lord departed out of his sight.*

^{22} *And when Gideon perceived that he was an angel of the Lord, Gideon said, Alas, O Lord God! for because I have seen an angel of the Lord face to face.*

^{23} *And the Lord said unto him, Peace be unto thee; fear not: thou shalt not die.*

Judges 6:11-23 (KJV)

This is one of the more descriptive and profound passages to show this idea of the other YHWH. Verses 11 and 12 tell us that this whole exchange was between Gideon and the angel of the Lord.[106] In verse 14, it switches and just says *"the Lord"*. Then, in verse 20, it switches back to *"the angel of the Lord"* and this angel actually accepts the offering that was meant for the Lord in verse 21, showing that the angel and the Lord are one in the same. Next, the angel disappears, which is when

---

[106] Also notice that it states *an* angel and *the* angel in reference to the same being. This further shows that there is no perfect formula or black and white explanation to show if an angel is YHWH or a regular angel. This is why we must always take things in context to know for sure.

Gideon puts it all together and realizes it was actually YHWH he was talking to. He is so surprised by this, in fact, he fears for his life. But then, as the ultimate mind-bender, YHWH tells Gideon to not be afraid; that he would not die. This, of course, was said *after* YHWH (as the angel of the Lord) disappeared. Not only was He there as two apparent manifestations, one seen and one unseen, but He also left without leaving, and remained without remaining. One can only wonder what such an exchange would have looked like from Gideon's perspective.

The Word

We have looked at a few examples of the name and the angel. Now, we can discover what the Bible has to say about *"the word"*. This is a term that should be familiar to all of us. The gospel of John opens up by explaining that the word is Jesus. Was this a term that John created himself, or was he building off an Old Testament teaching?

The very first appearance of the word of the Lord is described in the book of Genesis:

> [15:1] *After these things the word of the Lord came unto Abram in a vision, saying, Fear not, Abram: I am thy shield, and thy exceeding great reward.*
>
> [2] *And Abram said, Lord God, what wilt thou give me, seeing I go childless, and the steward of my house is this Eliezer of Damascus?*
>
> Genesis 15:1-2 (KJV)

It might make sense at first to think this is simply describing God's voice. However, keep in mind that verse 1 states this is a vision, meaning something Abram saw. Nothing else visual is described here; the only thing Abram could be seeing is the word. We are dealing with something more than just a voice. To show this further, consider these next passages:

And the child Samuel ministered unto the Lord before Eli. And the word of the Lord was precious in those days; there was no open vision.

1 Samuel 3:1 (KJV)

And the Lord came, and stood, and called as at other times, Samuel, Samuel. Then Samuel answered, Speak; for thy servant heareth.

1 Samuel 3:10 (KJV)

And the Lord appeared again in Shiloh: for the Lord revealed himself to Samuel in Shiloh by the word of the Lord.

1 Samuel 3:21 (KJV)

In all honesty, the entire third chapter of Samuel should be read through to get the full grasp of the message. However, we can use these three verses to show that the word of the Lord is not merely a voice, but is actually a visual manifestation of YHWH Himself.

In verse 1, we read that the word of the Lord was precious (that is to say, scarce) in those days. Then, by use of the semicolon to show it is further explaining the same point, it says there was no open vision. This is telling us that when the word of the Lord appeared, it would be through a vision, meaning something that can be seen. Next, in verse 10, we read that the Lord stood and called Samuel. This means the Lord was present while He was calling Samuel. This is not describing a disembodied voice (a voice lacks the ability to stand); this is describing YHWH Himself. Lastly, in verse 21, we read that the Lord revealed Himself by the word of the Lord. The word of the Lord was something Samuel was able to see. It is possible that YHWH uses these things, such as the angel, name, and word, so He can be in the presence of a person without that person losing their life through the experience.[107]

We can further prove the personification of the word by looking at three comparative verses from the first chapter of the book of Jeremiah:

Then the word of the Lord came unto me, saying,

Jeremiah 1:4 (KJV)

But the Lord said unto me, Say not, I am a child: for thou shalt go to all that I shall send thee, and whatsoever I command thee thou shalt speak.

Jeremiah 1:7 (KJV)

Then the Lord put forth his hand, and touched my mouth. And the Lord said unto me, Behold, I have put my words in thy mouth.

Jeremiah 1:9 (KJV)

In verse 4, we read that the word of the Lord came to Jeremiah. Verse 7 tells us that it is the Lord speaking, thereby confirming the word of the Lord and the Lord are the same. Then, in verse 9, we read that the Lord

---

[107] Exodus 33:20 tells us that we cannot see God face to face or we will die.

(also synonymous with the word of the Lord) put out His hand and touched Jeremiah's mouth. This shows that the word of the Lord has actual physical characteristics. If this were just a voice, these characteristics would not be present.

> *By the word of the Lord were the heavens made; and all the host of them by the breath of his mouth.*
>
> *Psalm 33:6 (KJV)*

This passage can confirm for us that the word of the Lord is actually YHWH Himself. This tells us that it was by *"the word of the Lord"* that the heavens were made. Then it makes mention of *"the breath of his mouth"*. A voice by itself does not possess breath or a mouth. This further shows the word of the Lord is YHWH and not only His voice.

The word of the Lord, going along with the idea of the second YHWH idea, is exactly who John was referring to in the beginning of chapter 1 of the gospel of John. John was not making up a new term; he was working from an Old Testament idea. This means it was YHWH Himself, the second YHWH, whether we call Him the angel, name, or word, who actually is Jesus Christ. It was this second YHWH, named Jesus Christ on the earth, who was slain on the cross for our sins. It was Jesus Christ who led His people out of Egyptian captivity. They are one in the same, yet distinct.

One other great example showing the relationship between Jesus and YHWH is found in the book of Psalms:

> [110:1] *The Lord said unto my Lord, Sit thou at my right hand, until I make thine enemies thy footstool.*

² The Lord shall send the rod of thy strength out of Zion: rule thou in the midst of thine enemies.

³ Thy people shall be willing in the day of thy power, in the beauties of holiness from the womb of the morning: thou hast the dew of thy youth.

⁴ The Lord hath sworn, and will not repent, Thou art a priest for ever after the order of Melchizedek.

⁵ The Lord at thy right hand shall strike through kings in the day of his wrath.

⁶ He shall judge among the heathen, he shall fill the places with the dead bodies; he shall wound the heads over many countries.

⁷ He shall drink of the brook in the way: therefore shall he lift up the head.

Psalm 110 (KJV)

This psalm is obviously speaking about Jesus, but look at how the first verse is worded. It says *"The Lord said unto my Lord"*. This could be translated in a number of ways from the Hebrew language, using names like YHWH and titles like Adonai, but the idea is the same. This is describing YHWH speaking to YHWH, both the same yet distinct.

The Spirit

We have seen examples from both the Old and New Testaments showing the complex relationship between YHWH and Jesus. You might be wondering where the Holy Spirit fits into all of this. There doesn't seem to be quite as much referencing the Holy Spirit, but it is there if we know where to look.

I will also add that, since YHWH and Jesus are the same yet distinct, it would stand to reason the Holy Spirit is the same yet distinct as well. There are times the angel and name are mentioned that could be referring to the Holy Spirit; essentially it is all YHWH anyway. For a bit more specification regarding the Holy Spirit, however, consider this passage:

> [8:1] *And it came to pass in the sixth year, in the sixth month, in the fifth day of the month, as I sat in mine house, and the elders of Judah sat before me, that the hand of the Lord God fell there upon me.*
>
> [2] *Then I beheld, and lo a likeness as the appearance of fire: from the appearance of his loins even downward, fire; and from his loins even upward, as the appearance of brightness, as the colour of amber.*
>
> [3] *And he put forth the form of an hand, and took me by a lock of mine head; and the spirit lifted me up between the earth and the heaven, and brought me in the visions of God to Jerusalem, to the door of the inner gate that looketh toward the north; where was the seat of the image of jealousy, which provoketh to jealousy.*
>
> *Ezekiel 8:1-3 (KJV)*

This is a bit more subtle, but it is there nonetheless. We read in verse 1 that the *"hand of the Lord"* fell upon Ezekiel. In verse 2, Ezekiel is describing the Lord, who, in verse 3, puts forth the form of a hand toward Ezekiel. Then something interesting happens. It says *"the spirit lifted me up between the earth and the heaven, and brought me in the visions of God".* Ezekiel was first describing the appearance of the Lord, then he switches to use the word *"spirit"*, while going back to the word *"God"* to describe the visions. By the language, it would seem as Ezekiel is describing three different Persons here. It is possible this is an Old Testament example of the Trinity.[108]

Throughout this chapter, we have seen many examples of the more obscure attributes of God. This can help us appreciate more His uniqueness, holiness, and majesty within His creation. Now when we consider strange phenomena in quantum mechanics, such as a particle existing in two places at once or popping in and out of existence, we can see how God's fingerprints are all over them. God embeds examples of Himself and His attributes into His creation. We have looked at many examples of this throughout this book, but there is one major example we have yet to explore. Did God embed any of His more obscure and unique nature in His creation of humanity?

---

[108] There are many, many more examples we could have looked at in this study. For more information in this idea of a second YHWH, I would highly recommend the extensive work of Dr. Michael Heiser. He has written about this in the past and has a few presentations on YouTube. At the time of this writing, the one I would recommend most can be found here: http://youtu.be/Hz8J4DTIkEg - entitled *The Jewish Trinity*.

Chapter 11

Dual Citizenship across Time and Space

*Even when we were dead in sins, hath quickened us together with
Christ, (by grace ye are saved;) And hath raised us up together, and
made us sit together in heavenly places in Christ Jesus:*

Ephesians 2:5-6 (KJV)

An Often Overlooked Passage

The passage quoted above is one of profound importance, though it may not seem so upon first read. Many times, with passages such as this, we tend to get the main idea and read ahead while glossing over what could be important details. Verses such as these can seem simple on the surface, yet much can be learned from a deeper study.

Though I have been quoting from the King James Version of the Bible throughout this entire book, I think it would be of benefit to study this verse from the New King James Version:

[2:5] *Even when we were dead in trespasses, made us alive together
with Christ (by grace you have been saved),*

⁶ and raised us up together, and made us sit together in the heavenly places in Christ Jesus,

Ephesians 2:5-6 (NKJV)

The reason I propose the New King James Version translation over the King James Version translation is it makes our study a bit simpler to grasp without changing the meaning of the passage.

Many times, when this passage is interpreted, it is taught that Jesus sees us *as if* we are already seated with Him. But is this what the text actually says? The text teaches this principal in past tense, portraying the fact that this has already happened. When we *were* dead, He *made* us alive together with Christ, and *raised* us up, and *made* us sit together in the heavenly places in Christ Jesus. This is all past tense. If we have accepted Jesus as our Savior, this is already done. What exactly does that mean for us as Christians?

This is usually looked at as a nice metaphor or a clever way to explain a certain principle. Many times, in cases such as these, there can usually be found a deeper truth with further study. This passage could very well be more literal than we might originally think. When we look at it closely, we realize very direct and literal language is used. We do not see *as if* or *like* anywhere in the passage. It is directly saying that a literal event occurred when you and I accepted Jesus Christ as our Savior. We were literally seated in Heaven with Jesus.

The Greek word used for the idea of us being raised together comes from *"synegeirō"*, meaning:

"1. to raise together, to cause to raise together

2. to raise up together from mortal death to a new and blessed life dedicated to God".[109]

From this, we can realize that we were, in a sense, born into death, but since we accepted Jesus' gift of salvation, we have been raised and seated in Heaven. Also notice that this happened to all of us *together*, implicating that it happened within the same instant.

What we are dealing with here is the same event in at least two separate dimensions, possibly more. We have discussed the possibility of extra dimensions existing. It seems that whichever dimension describes Heaven is the context of this passage. The physical and spiritual dimensions are what Ephesians 2:5-6 is dealing with.

In the three physical dimensions we can experience here on Earth, we accept Jesus as our Savior and begin our new life. In the spiritual dimension, in Heaven, it is something far more profound than we realize. This goes back to the idea that time may operate differently in Heaven. Every three-dimensional, physical thing is stuck within the confines of time. Because of this, time is our reality. The spiritual dimension, however, might be different. Time could be more fluid there. God, in essence, is outside of time. He can manipulate time as He sees fit (such as to allow John to feel the passage of about half an hour's time during his vision in Revelation 8), but God Himself is, by nature, outside of time. He would have to be. If He weren't, if God was stuck in time

---

[109] "Greek Lexicon :: G4891 (KJV)." Blue Letter Bible. Accessed 1 June, 2014.
http://www.blueletterbible.org/lang/Lexicon/Lexicon.cfm?Strongs=G4891&t=KJV

with the rest of us, it would mean there was a power or force higher than God Himself. Such a thing is Biblically impossible. Time is just another one of God's creations.

The way this idea can apply to Ephesians 2:5-6 is quite interesting. The passage seems to be saying that we as Christians are *already* in Heaven. Right now, as you are reading this, if you are secure in Jesus, you are already seated with Jesus in Heaven. Now, of course, this is something that is occurring in a spiritual dimension. This is something outside of the physical timeline. We cannot apply this to our physical lives and think we can do whatever we want because it is already done in Heaven. That is not at all what the passage is suggesting. If anything, it should prove the exact opposite.

We started off in this life as dead in our sins, beginning at least after the age of accountability. If we had continued down that path and had never accepted Jesus, we would be dead already, even though we would still be physically alive. That is what the beginning of the passage in Ephesians is signifying. Accepting the gift of salvation takes us out of the spiritual state of death and raises us to life with Jesus Christ outside of knowable time and space. Even if we could, we should not want to return to the same sinful life that was keeping us in a state of perpetual death.

Because this is a question that might come up, I will state that I do not believe this is suggesting we existed in Heaven before we were born. In my humble opinion, there are many problems with that theory. First, for there to be a *before*, there would have to be physical *time*. That does not seem to work with God in the spiritual dimension. When it comes to God at least, there is no before. There is no after. There just *is*. Now again, God can manipulate time as He sees fit. However, for us as physical humans, we do not have access to anything beyond physical time while in physical existence. When we shed our physicality and are on the other side, then we can experience that sort of fluid time/timelessness. But as long as we exist in physical reality, we can't.

Also, we were born into a sinful world and into sinful bodies. Our physical and spiritual existence began at the same time. We were not born into eternity. But, when we accepted Jesus, we were lifted into eternity, outside of knowable time and space, to be seated with Jesus where we are now. To show this biblically, consider the fact that when God created Adam, He breathed into him the breath of life. Adam then became a living soul.[110] This means he was not a living soul beforehand. Adam did not exist in Heaven before he was created on Earth. His physical being and spiritual being were created at the same time, both here on Earth. Such is the same for each one of us.

While it is a difficult thing to contemplate, the Bible makes it clear that when we were saved, we were lifted into Heaven. This indicates that we are already there. In a sense, this seems to convey the idea that we are in two places at once, though we would not normally realize it without revelation from God through the Bible. I also believe this explains how we can be sealed eternally.[111] Biblically speaking, eternity does not seem to describe an expanse of time, but more of a state of existence, almost a type of spiritual location. We are sealed because

---

[110] Genesis 2:7
[111] Ephesians 1:13

we are already there. This could also explain why nothing can take us out of God's hands. With God, it is already done.

What is also interesting is it says we were raised together. This also adds to the theory of us already being there. Because God is outside of knowable time, when I was saved and when you were saved, we were raised together. We were also raised together with the apostle Paul when he accepted Jesus as his Savior.

In physical, three-dimensional reality, we can point to a specific time when we were saved. However, on the other side, it is all the same and we share in it together. Three-dimensional space and time have no bearing concerning Heaven and the construct of the higher dimensions. Time does seem to exist, at least to a certain degree, but God Himself is outside of His own construct of time and space in all dimensions.

There is much that can be considered and many questions that can be asked concerning this. For example, when John was caught up to Heaven and given his vision of the Revelation, he saw people that would be slain for their testimony in Jesus. When those people are slain in our future, will they personally witness John having his vision roughly 2,000 years prior?

Also, there is a theory that states the 24 elders in Revelation were the 12 apostles and 12 sons of Jacob. If this is true, when John saw the elders, did he see himself? Are there more examples of experiences through time and dimensional space that can be examined within the pages of our Bibles?

CHAPTER 11

The answer is, I really don't know. Much of this is theoretical and even speculative. At the very least, this is an interesting thought concerning, what I consider to be, a biblical truth. We can see how God included examples of His qualities in His creation. Also, it does seem that God has embedded the potential for His obscure qualities of dual existence within each and every one of us. We just need to accept Jesus as our Savior to partake in these qualities ourselves.

If this whole idea presented within this chapter is true, it shows us even more of the sheer beauty and majesty of YHWH, our Lord Almighty. I don't believe any of us will fully know the ultimate depths of this idea until it is time to escape our own physical existence. In my deepest hope and sincerest belief, it will be then that each one of us who have found our salvation in Jesus Christ will wake up together, see our Lord, and finally realize for ourselves that we have been there the whole time.

About the Author

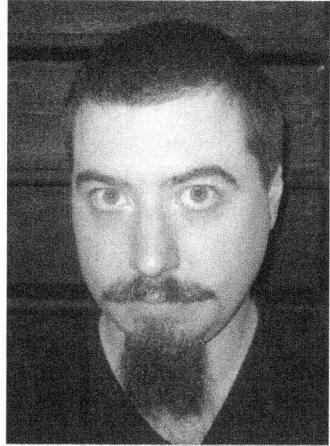

Josh Peck is a Christian author and biblical researcher. He works toward waking up the Church to the reality of the Bible, separating biblical truth from Church tradition when necessary, and providing the solid, raw, and uncut truth of God's Word to any and all who are interested. He is the founder of Ministudy Ministry, the goal of which is to provide short, personal, and inexpensive study materials for the average at-home Bible reader, study group, and church. Josh Peck also hosts a weekly audio and video internet show entitled The Sharpening, which features regular guests and Bible study covering a wide range of topics. All past audio and video episodes of The Sharpening can be found at www.youtube.com/joshpeckdisclosure. All past as well as upcoming audio episodes of The Sharpening can be found at www.blogtalkradio.com/thesharpening. For more information Josh Peck, Ministudy Ministry, and The Sharpening, visit www.ministudyministry.com.

Other Titles by Josh Peck

Available at MinistudyMinistry.com

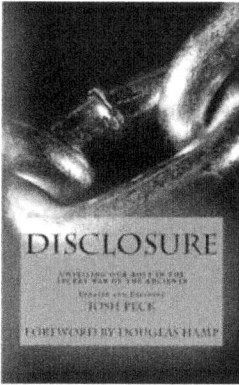

DISCLOSURE - UPDATED
AND EXPANDED

Unveiling Our Role in the Secret War of the Ancients

Updated and Expanded

Foreword by Douglas Hamp

There is a war against humanity that has been raging for nearly six thousand years. The Great Commander, Jesus Christ, has set up His Church to fight the enemy. The problem is the enemy has convinced the Church that the war does not exist.

Many Christians today are unknowingly being hidden away from true Bible prophecy. Disclosure answers this problem by guiding a Christian through even the most traditional beliefs to the exciting world of God's promises and prophecy, including topics such as the Nephilim and the green horse of Revelation. There has never been a more important time in history for the Church to be informed. The enemy is setting the stage for the greatest deception the world has ever seen. Disclosure sorts out truth from tradition and digs out the hidden prophecies that God has left for us in His Word.

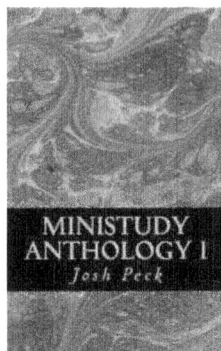

MINISTUDY ANTHOLOGY I

Welcome to the first collection of Ministudy Books by author Josh Peck! Included are the first five Ministudy books ever produced by Ministudy Ministry. You will never again find a collection that offers so much biblical information that can lead you to a closer relationship with God and His Son Jesus Christ.

Titles include: The Four Degrees of Baptism, Spiritual Warfare against the Satanic Government, The Day of the Lord, Sorting Out the Resurrection and Ascensions of Christ, and What Loving God Really Means (previously unreleased title).

Plus extra bonus writings by Josh Peck!

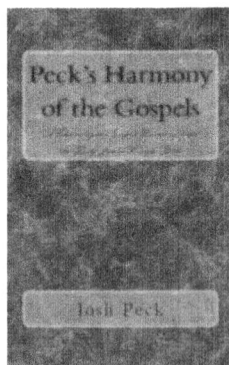

PECK'S HARMONY OF THE GOSPELS

A Chronological Gospel Harmony from the King James Version Bible

Get ready to experience the Gospels like never before! The idea behind this Gospel Harmony is to blend the four Gospels into a single, coherent, and chronological narrative. This provides a clearer picture and appreciation for the life of Jesus; what He did, when He did it, and what it means for all of us today. This Gospel Harmony is a wonderful tool for personal study and enjoyment of the first four books of the New Testament taken from the King James Version of the Holy Bible.

In the past, there have been many wonderful attempts at harmonizing the four Gospels. There are many features of this Gospel Harmony that are not found in any other:

- Gospels separated by font-emphasis instead of parallel columns for a great reading experience (Matthew in regular text, Mark in underlined text, Luke in italic text, and John in bold text);
- Chronological order;
- Verse number included for every verse;
- Chapter and verse number references for every time the Gospel or section changes;
- A Table of Contents of large sections in the front of the book;
- A Table of Contents of small sections in the back of the book;

And much more!

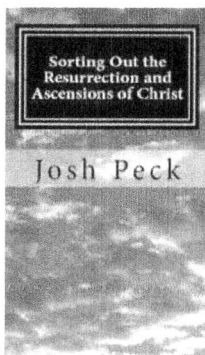

SORTING OUT THE RESURRECTION AND ASCENISONS OF CHRIST

A Ministudy Ministry Book

What is the proper order of events for Jesus' resurrection? Is it possible to put the events of Jesus' life after death into chronological order? Why are there so many apparent contradictions within the four Gospels?

Using "Peck's Harmony of the Gospels" as a tool for understanding, Josh Peck answers these questions and more in "Sorting Out the Resurrection and Ascensions of Christ". Find out how to answer the difficult questions concerning the details of the four Gospels. Discover the proper order of the events surrounding Jesus' resurrection. Learn exactly how many times Jesus ascended into Heaven. This is a book you will not want to miss!

THE DAY OF THE LORD

A Ministudy Ministry Book

What exactly is the Day of the Lord? When will it occur? Does Church tradition differ from biblical fact concerning the Day of the Lord? What is the difference between the Day of the Lord and the rapture? What are we in store for and how should we prepare? Are there misconceptions being taught today about the Day of the Lord, and if so, what is the truth? What does the Bible really teach? Josh Peck answers these questions and many more in "The Day of the Lord". Discover the surprising truth about this amazing day and how it will affect you as a Christian. Learn what you should do to prepare and how to guard against deception. Gain specific knowledge pertaining to the common misinterpretations regarding the Day of the Lord. Through this important revelation of truth, you will be left with information that will guard you against false teachings and bring you into a closer relationship with God.

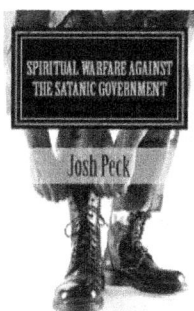

SPIRITUAL WARFARE AGAINST THE SATANIC GOVERNMENT

A Ministudy Ministry Book

What does the Bible say about spiritual warfare? What weapons are given to us by God? Who is our true enemy? Is it possible to be more powerful than evil spirits? How can we claim victory over Satan? Josh Peck answers all these questions and more in "Spiritual Warfare against the Satanic Government". Learn everything about the true enemy of the Church, including how you can claim authority over them. Find out how to go through life without fear, no matter what hardships might come along. Discover the true power of the Holy Spirit given to all Christians by God Himself. In this enlightening book, you will realize your full potential in Jesus Christ by learning what it means to be a true and mighty warrior for His Church.

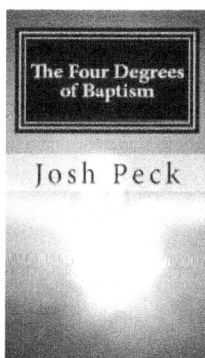

THE FOUR DEGREES OF BAPTISM

A Ministudy Ministry Book

What is the meaning of true and complete baptism? Is there more to It than submersion in water? What does the Bible have to say about baptism as a whole? Josh Peck answers these questions and more in "The Four Degrees of Baptism". Learn what the four degrees are, their prophetic importance, and how to embrace them all. The understanding provided in this short teaching will pave the way toward a closer relationship with God.

Contributing Authors

S. Douglas Woodward: www.faith-happens.com

Dr. Ken Johnson: www.biblefacts.org

Dr. Ronald Mallett: www.uconn.edu

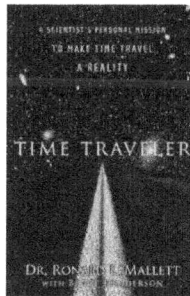

.

Lightning Source UK Ltd.
Milton Keynes UK
UKOW05f1833240417
299813UK00010B/510/P